JON TEEL

Lana Laws Downing

ISBN 978-1-64258-215-4 (paperback)
ISBN 978-1-64258-216-1 (digital)

Christian Faith Publishing, Inc.
832 Park Avenue
Meadville, PA 16335
www.christianfaithpublishing.com

This is a work of fiction. All characters and events portrayed are products of the author's imagination, or are used fictitiously.

Printed in the United States of America

Dedication

To Trent, for constant encouragement and unfailing support.

Contents

The Mystery Boy

August heat shimmered in waves above the cracked asphalt path through the cemetery. Julia willed herself to stand tall as perspiration trickled down her back. Her hair was wet under the flowered straw hat she had bought for the occasion, bowing to the fashion dictates of the women of St. Matthew Zion First Bible Church. Her right hand rested on the bony shoulder of Jon Teel. As she patted him gently, he moved closer to her. "There is nowhere else on God's green Earth that I would rather be," she thought.

The small wood frame church on Bayou Bend Road had been packed for the funeral service, but there were few mourners at the cemetery. Reverend Wylie Pritchard was known for his lengthy graveside eulogies. Today, he did not disappoint, his honey-thick baritone extolling the virtues of a woman who had fostered countless children in her tidy home near the old train depot. Jon Teel, standing beside Julia, was one of her most recent charges. His small body shuddered, but Julia saw no tears.

Local fascination with Jon Teel ran high when he first appeared in Bakerville. He had arrived in Lafayette on a Greyhound bus from Houston. A woman was with him from Houston to Beaumont, but when the bus arrived in Lafayette, no passenger could remember what the woman looked like or when she had left the bus. Jon Teel had slept through her departure. The only clue to the boy's identity was a note pinned to his shirt that read: "My name is Jon Teel. Send me to Auntie Jones, Sycamore Street, Bakerville, LA."

A local television reporter happened to be at the bus station in Lafayette on the Saturday evening when the bus carrying Jon Teel arrived.

The reporter was covering the plight of the many homeless, both men and women, who frequently took shelter in the station. As it became apparent that the boy had been abandoned somewhere between Beaumont and Lafayette, the station attendant came to the bus at the direction of the driver. The two removed the sleepy child, and then called police. The television reporter directed the cameraman to film nonstop until the child was whisked away in the police cruiser. The drama was captured in its entirety by the television cameraman. The reporter knew television gold when he saw it happening, and this was it. The privacy of a minor child did not enter his head, or, worse, if it did, it did not concern him.

Because the events unfolded on a weekend, it was Monday by the time the Department of Children and Family Services became aware of the airing of the story and forced the local station to pull the footage. The damage had been done. Airing such footage of a child was against all departmental policies. The weekend crew at the television station was not well-versed on protecting identities of minors. Although the station quickly pulled the story and issued an apology once they were contacted, it was too late. What had been seen could not be unseen. Jon Teel's poignant, pinched face and haunted eyes had captured the hearts of Acadiana. The reporter narrated the story of the lost boy, while video depicted the small, wide-eyed child as a police officer helped him into the back of a big cruiser for the ride to Bakerville.

The boy was little help in locating his family when he was delivered to the doctor and the sheriff awaiting him at the Bakerville hospital, replying to questions about his name with the mumbled reply, "My name is Jon Teel."

In an examination room at the hospital, Dr. Elias Christian looked across the top of Jon Teel's head, raising his eyebrows at the sheriff. The child's back was mottled with scars, apparently from cigarette burns. His wrists and neck were encircled with raised welts. Both the doctor and the sheriff had seen abused children, but Jon Teel was the worst either of the men had witnessed. And they had not yet viewed his X-rays. The sheriff had little hope that the mystery boy would be claimed. No one would come forward to admit to the horrific criminal offenses the child had suffered. On the other hand, thanks to the Lafayette reporter, the story of the boy had been broadcast far and wide, so there was scant hope of keeping his presence in Bakerville a secret should someone come looking for him.

The boy stoically submitted to the doctor's examination but offered no answers. Eyes cast down, expressionless, he made himself as unobtrusive as possible.

"How did this mark get on your wrist, Jon Teel?" The doctor was gentle with his question, but he was required to ask. The boy shrugged his shoulders in reply.

The most mysterious of his injuries was the absence of the little finger on his left hand. It had healed over, obviously without medical attention, leaving a tiny stump covered with scarred flesh. When asked about the injury, he shrugged his shoulders and murmured, "Beast," but nothing more. While Jon Teel waited in the examination room, the doctor and sheriff conferred behind closed doors.

"Doc, I gotta tell you. I am going to have nightmares for a long time over what I just saw in there," Sheriff Joe Blanchard said.

"I must admit," the gentle doctor replied, "it is the worst case I have seen in my career. I would like five minutes alone with the monster who did this to that innocent boy."

"We know the boy boarded the bus in Houston. I have been in touch with the sheriff in Harris County, Texas. He has some ideas, but he says we have to tread carefully. If what he suspects is true, this ties in with some really bad hombres involved in the Houston drug trade. The unfortunate television coverage is going to make it hard to keep quiet, but at least we have kept Auntie Jones' name out of the news. We have to keep the boy safe. I can't imagine anyone showing up to claim him given that they are sure to be arrested on sight, but you never know what some of those drug lords are capable of doing. They think they are above the law." This was a long speech for the normally taciturn sheriff.

"You stay on top of keeping the boy out of harm's way, and I will tend to his physical injuries free of charge," the doctor replied.

"In the meantime, I will take him over to Auntie Jones and see if she has room. This is our only real clue, and it isn't much to go on."

He held out the rumpled note from the boy's shirt, safety pin still attached, encased in a clear plastic evidence bag. They had decided to keep everything the boy had with him in evidence: an extra pair of ragged underwear, the note about Auntie Jones, and two very tattered old children's books, library discards from Harris County, Texas.

"I believe I will ask Auntie to keep him at home as much as possible and not to let on that she has him. I want to keep him as safe as we can manage. He will have to be enrolled in school, but we already have a deputy assigned there."

Silver Spoon

Julia Chandler Hancock stood in the back sunroom of her expansive home gazing down at the Bayou Teche, a milk chocolate stream moving sluggishly along the sinuous track that gave it the Chitimacha name for snake. What was it about small southern towns, Julia wondered, that made them stay the same the more they changed? This town was like the bayou: moving slowly, not easily persuaded from its path, shallow in most places but deep in others. And as thoroughly murky as the intricacies of Bakerville's lore and history, both the true and the fabricated.

Julia polished a Francis I nut spoon, placed it in a crystal dish, and glanced out toward the bayou once again, this time marveling at the beauty of newly cleaned glass windows, Florida's handiwork. Flo was a firm believer in polished glass and gleaming silver. What would she do without Florida? A fixture in the household, Florida was more an older sister to Julia than she was an employee. Her mother had come to work for Judge Chandler before Julia was born, living in a small house on the property. There was a story to the coming of Florida and her family. Of that fact, Julia was certain. If her mother had known it, she had taken the knowledge with her to her grave. Florida had been Julia's first friend; they were inseparable playmates when they were young, and they remained fast friends. Florida could bring Julia back to reality when her emotions got the best of her.

Only once had Julia and Florida come close to discussing the issue of their family connection. Some years back, shortly after the death of Julia's husband John, Julia had come into the formal living room to find Florida gazing at the portrait of Julia's great-great-grandfather, an intrepid sea captain. It was he who had built Dapplefield Manor in the mid-1800s. He was a naval captain who made a fortune in sea trade, hauling lumber, sugar, and fur to northern ports and bringing back manufactured goods and necessities of life from north to south.

In the portrait, he wore his naval uniform. His face was turned in partial profile, one hand tucked into his uniform front and the other holding a brass telescope. Julia loved the portrait of her ancestor. For the first time, though, seeing Florida gazing up at the portrait, unaware of Julia's presence, Julia was thunderstruck at the resemblance between the handsome woman of color and the aristocratic sea captain, Nathaniel Smith Chandler. Their profiles were identical. In addition, the set of the jaw and the cheekbones, everything except the skin tone and eye color, were eerily similar.

"Flo," Julia began, "I never noticed before how much you look like my old great-great-grandpa."

Florida jumped as though a cannon had gone off in the room.

"Julia, that is the craziest thing I ever heard. If you value our friendship you will never speak of such a thing again. Never."

With that, the subject was closed. Julia knew that Florida knew, and Florida now knew that Julia knew, but if Florida did not want to acknowledge her lineage, the least Julia could do was honor her wishes. The irony of it all was not lost on Julia.

*   *   *   *   *

Julia's card-playing group was coming for the afternoon, repeating a ritual begun by her grandmother in the 1920s when her grandfather, the first Judge Chandler, built the beautiful open sunroom at the back of the old antebellum mansion.

Her mother regaled her with the story many times. The town was evenly divided over whether or not the room should be built. Some felt it destroyed the architectural integrity of the finest old home in town. Others thought it fitting that the house be brought into the twentieth century. "Sunroom" conjured up visions of Europe in the minds of others. No one dared voice an opinion to the judge, but Julia's grandmother heard about it on the street. The judge, accustomed to brooking no interference or criticism, went ahead with his plan, taking off the back gallery and replacing it with a glassed-in room that went across the entire back side of the house, extending out sixteen feet. Polished wood floors covered with Persian rugs, white wicker furniture, and ceiling fans created a space that was beautiful and inviting. The northeast exposure made for pleasant afternoons. The gently undulating lawn went down to the bayou, where there was a small covered dock. The view from the sunroom was incomparable.

Here the card games had begun three quarters of a century ago, and here they continued today. Three of Julia's card-playing friends were granddaughters of the original group of players. How many decisions had been made, marriages had ended or been saved, and secrets had been shared over the card tables? Julia loved carrying on the tradition, still using plates and silver her grandmother had used all those years ago. She polished one last silver teaspoon, smiling at the obvious symbolism. She really had been born with a silver spoon in her mouth.

Julia poured a second cup of coffee and walked over to the big carved buffet. She opened the lid of an old cypress wood box, reached in, and drew out a scrap of paper. She unfolded it and read the faded flowing script: "Follow the words of St. James. Guard your tongue today." Knowing the gin players were coming, Julia decided it was a perfect opportunity to try to follow the sage advice.

The habit of choosing a scrap of paper from the old box of wise sayings was a family tradition begun before Julia's ancestors came down the Ohio River on a flat barge. They had traveled down the Mississippi, winding their way through the bayous to make a claim on property along Bayou Teche in the early 1800s. The original box of wise sayings was lost on the arduous trip, falling overboard and floating away in a storm. The current box, built of virgin cypress wood with peg construction, was made before the family built their first home. The date "1808" was carved into the bottom of the box. Bible quotes, newspaper blurbs, handwritten sayings, and all manner of good advice, religious and otherwise, had been added through the years, until the box was crammed full. Julia pulled out a saying at least once a day, sometimes more. She planned to remove all the papers to preserve by typing them on her computer, but that particular someday had not yet arrived.

Next, she picked up the Lafayette newspaper. She had a ritual in her newspaper reading. She read the front-page news, and then she turned to the obituaries. Julia, though not a morbid person, loved the obituaries. She collected the humorous ones. Her favorite one of late was that of a woman from a nearby town. It declared that she had "loved her friends and family, country music, playing cards, and running the back roads." How, Julia mused, would she even begin to run the back roads? She wouldn't know where to start. Maybe taking on such a daring habit would liven up her increasingly predictable life.

The television carried the noon news. Julia picked up the remote and turned up the volume, hoping to catch an update on the boy from the bus station. The story had broken two nights ago, and Julia had been haunted ever since by the eyes of the tiny child looking out from the back seat of a police cruiser. He had arrived in Lafayette on a Greyhound bus from Houston. A woman was with him from Houston to Beaumont, but when the bus arrived in Lafayette, no passenger could remember what the woman looked like or when she had left the bus. The boy had slept through her departure.

Julia was disappointed when the story of the lost boy was not mentioned. Julia replayed in her mind the video of the small, wide-eyed child as a police officer helped him into the back of a big cruiser with a wire panel caging off the back seat. The boy was little help in locating his family, replying to questions about his name with the mumbled reply, "My name is Jon Teel," but nothing more. Julia mulled over in her mind her many contacts in the area who might shed light on the child and his plight. She firmed up her resolve to learn what she could and to do what she could to help the child.

*   *   *   *   *

Unbeknownst to Julia, she was already involved in the saga of young Jon Teel. At the September meeting of Techeland Chapter of the Daughters of the American Revolution, the members welcomed a newcomer, Marley something or other, whose husband ran the business office for the gas company. Marley was from Alabama and positively brimming over with enthusiasm. The regent, not one to waste energetic new blood in the group, asked her to take over the literacy committee. When new business was called for, Marley spoke right up.

"Ladies, the promotion of literacy for our very young students is a calling, a vocation for all of us. If we do not encourage a literate population, we have no hope for the future. All I am asking is one hour per week from any of you who are willing to give that time to go into our school libraries and work with an elementary student. There is no substitute for one-on-one attention."

Her impassioned plea struck a chord with Julia, who had a PhD in education with emphasis on language arts. She had taught at a nearby university until her marriage. She recognized the truth of the young woman's words.

Raising her hand, she spoke up, "I would be delighted to tutor a student one hour each week."

"Oh, thank you, Mrs. Hancock! You are our very first volunteer!"

A few other hands were raised, a list made, and Marley said she would present the list to the school board office where it would be examined and approved by the reading supervisor and a schedule drawn up. Julia promptly forgot about it, because she knew the wheels of any government-related body turned slowly and the schools were no exception.

Julia decided that she would call her long-time friend Judge Porteus Green, the head of juvenile court in the judicial district that included Bakerville, the parish seat, to express her interest in the child Jon Teel. The unclaimed boy had firmly fixed himself in her mind; she couldn't shake the feeling that she was meant to help him. Meanwhile, she had card players arriving, expecting to be entertained.

The Gin Bunch

The doorbell chimed. Julia opened the door to a flurry of women bearing huge purses, dishes of food, and clinking bags of change for their elaborate albeit paltry betting. Margot Rienzi Berchamp, Jane Bell Smith, Louella dela Fonze Hill, and the only unmarried member of the group, Myrtle Cramer, formed the entering entourage. As exasperating as each of them could be, each would have given a kidney or a limb for any of the others. They were lifelong friends.

Since there were five attending today and only four could play, Myrtle appointed herself captain and went off to the kitchen with her culinary contribution and soon was cackling away with Florida. The other four paired off, and the gin game began.

Today there were two card tables. Julia played first against Margot, while Jane and Louella paired off. When six players attended, they had three tables, and the play became more intricate. They had played together three or four afternoons a week for so many years that the progression of the game was automatic. They played for money, but the winnings never totaled over $50. It was the conversation that they enjoyed much more than the play.

"Did you hear that Rena really did kick Gregory out?" Louella said.

"No!" Margot was incredulous. "She told Sylvia they had an agreement. He would provide the house and a good income for her, and she would look the other way regarding his shenanigans, and they would present a united front for the holidays for their daughters and grandchildren."

"I think that last stunt he pulled was the straw that broke the camel's back," Jane said, "and I know he has bought a big piece of property out on Bayou Bend Road and plans to build. But we hadn't ought to discuss the problems of our friends, and we don't know that it's true."

"I live across the street from them, and I saw Gregory leave with a suitcase," Margot commented uncomfortably. Her own husband was known to stray, always with the same woman and sometimes much too publicly, "So I for one believe it."

The players shuffled the cards and dealt round after round.

"If you snider me one more time, I swear I'm gonna quit," Louella said to Jane. Louella was known to ask for repayment if a friend borrowed a postage stamp. Losing $5.00 put her in a bad humor.

Myrtle came in from the kitchen to assume her duties as captain. She tallied up the boxes and gave the totals. Louella was behind by $7.35 and they were only halfway through the game.

"I think the sun is over the yardarm," she said. "I'm gonna fix a rum and Coke. Julia, do you have any lemon?"

"Isn't it a little bit early?" This was from Jane, who tried in vain to keep the group on the straight and narrow.

"Jane, you have a drink when you want one and I'll do the same," Louella replied.

Jane's Russian accent was more pronounced as she became agitated. She had been adopted as a young teenager after World War II, too late to acquire the nuances of unaccented American English.

"Louella, you have a drink. But we still have more rounds to play so you can win your money back, and you want to keep a clear head," Jane's accented tone was conciliatory.

Myrtle came in from the kitchen followed by a beaming Florida.

"Our English Tea is served in the breakfast room," she announced in obvious anticipation of exclamations of delight over their joint efforts.

Conversation over the delicious food soon turned to the mystery boy.

"Julia," Margot asked," do you have any news about him from your buddy Judge Green?"

"As a matter of fact," Julia replied, "I was thinking of calling him today to see if there is anything I can do for the child."

"Now, Julia," Louella said, "please do *not* tell me you are thinking of involving yourself in the life of an abused, orphaned, biracial child! I can't think of anything worse. Send a check to St. Jude Hospital if you have the urge to be altruistic. But don't get caught up in this. It could be dangerous! Somebody hurt that child, and they may want him back to finish what they started!"

To Julia's surprise, none of the others argued with Louella but instead seemed to give tacit approval to her strong words. Instead of deterring Julia, it only strengthened her resolve to try to help the child. She bit her tongue and did not reply, but now she was on a mission.

Julia Takes Action

The day after her card party, Julia continued to watch for any news of the mystery boy with the undernourished, scarred body, but there was a total blackout of information on the story. She still felt something akin to an electric shock when she remembered the split second when his eyes met the television camera turned on him. Julia had never seen such eyes. They were dark wells of the deepest despair. They looked exactly like she imagined the eyes of Jesus would be. No child should have eyes filled with such sadness. The feeling stayed with her.

Later, she realized she had not taken her daily wise saying from the box. She reached in and pulled out a piece of heavy cardstock on which was printed, "Live every day as though it were your last on Earth." She resolved then and there to connect somehow with the boy Jon Teel. Her best bet was Auntie Jones.

She knew from the news reports that Jon Teel had come to Bakerville. She also knew that the most likely placement of the boy would be with her old friend Auntie Jones. She knew she could not ask Auntie outright because the rules forbade Auntie from revealing anything about the children in her care. Julia decided to be a tiny bit duplicitous. She telephoned and asked Auntie how the mystery child was doing and if he needed anything. Auntie confirmed that the boy was living with her, but the authorities were trying to keep it quiet.

Julia had come to respect Auntie Jones through her CASA work; some of the children she worked with had resided with Auntie while they were assigned to Julia and her husband. She had great respect for Auntie's natural ability to work with profoundly disturbed young people. Julia could ascribe it only to Auntie's innate and genuine love for all children, even those who came to her kicking and screaming and yelling the worst obscenities imaginable. Auntie had a calming manner that soon worked its way with most of her young charges.

Julia and her husband had first gotten to know Auntie Jones when they had taken their CASA training together, meeting for regular sessions at the CASA office on a side street in Bakerville for wide-ranging classes on dealing with abused and abandoned children, their families, the courts, and other aspects of helping with the burgeoning number of young people thrown on the mercy of the courts and the "system." CASA volunteers, Court Appointed Special Advocates, were an important link in helping juvenile court judges gauge what was happening—or not happening—in the quest to find permanent, loving homes for society's youngest victims and to assure that their rights and well-being were protected and promoted.

Julia and John were taking the course to become certified CASA volunteers. Auntie Jones was taking the course in order to better serve the foster children in her care. She had been a nurse in the local hospital for many years, where she showed a gift with pediatric patients. When she retired, she decided to use those skills to become a foster parent. She had never married, so this course of action was a way to use her training and also have a family—a win-win. Julia, John, and Auntie Jones became fast friends over the course of the weeks of study, and the friendship was cemented when some of the Hancocks' CASA children happened to reside with Auntie Jones.

*   *   *   *   *

Julia decided to do some shopping for the young mystery boy. She estimated from the televised images that he was a size five or six. She would purchase an assortment of items and take them over to Auntie's home. This she did, arriving at Auntie's door early on a Monday afternoon.

"Julia, you are most kind. That child needs all the help and attention he can get. He is over at the school, but he is not doing so well. And I fear for his safety. What was done to that child ought to be punishable by death!" This was strong language from the soft-spoken Auntie, who rarely shared information about her charges. With Julia, she made an exception, revealing some of Jon Teel's injuries.

Julia had secretly hoped to catch a glimpse of Jon Teel, but that was not to be. She left the clothing with Auntie, but still felt herself even more drawn to the mystery child, compelled to learn about him, wondering how he could be salvaged after the horrific cruelty that had been inflicted on his tiny body. How could such an abuser be counted as a member of the human race?

It was at times like this that Julia most missed her husband John. They had married late in life; Julia was forty, John nearing sixty. John would be filled with sound, practical ideas for helping young Jon Teel. He would want to do anything in his power to salvage the life of the pitiful boy. For the time being, Julia fretted helplessly, not knowing what more she could do.

*   *   *   *   *

For several days, Julia discarded one idea after another for injecting herself into the life of the child. Then fate in the plump form of Judge

Porteous Green intervened. He summoned Julia to the courthouse to meet with him on a "special matter." Julia, assuming it had to do with her CASA work, presented herself a few minutes early for the appointment.

"Julia," the judge began, "we have been friends for a long time, since I was a young law student that your late father, God rest his soul, took under his wing, and you were a graduate student in New Orleans. Where have the years gone? But that is not what I called you here to discuss. I am sure you have seen the news about the young mystery child who came in on the bus with nothing to his name except a Walmart sack with an extra pair of ragged drawers, a couple of books, and a note with Auntie Jones's name and address. He is now enrolled in kindergarten over at the elementary school near you. He is making little to no progress. I have seen the short list of tutoring volunteers the ladies of the DAR turned in to the school board, and your name jumped right up and bit me. Would you consent to work with the child and see if you can somehow reach him? I know reading and the language arts are your bailiwick, and I also know that you have an empathetic way with children."

How could he possibly know that? Julia wondered but did not speak the thought. She supposed it was from her CASA work, which frequently took her to Judge Green's courtroom.

"He's just buttering me up," she thought. "He just doesn't realize how much I would love to try to help the child."

Julia did not hesitate; she readily agreed to work with Jon Teel.

First, she called on her professor buddies at the college in Lafayette, borrowing textbooks and journals filled with articles on the sad subject of child abuse. She was well-versed from her CASA work, but she could not afford any missteps. She read all that she could digest, deciding that common sense was the best approach. Do not force yourself on the child, allow the child to make moves at his own pace, let him know that anything he wants to say is okay, or if he wants to say nothing at all, that is okay, too.

The Work Begins

The day had come. Julia had gone to her stored teaching materials in the attic. She selected a few books, some wooden blocks, and a small metal tray that held brightly colored magnetic alphabet letters. Julia chose her outfit with care. She decided to wear a pantsuit that would allow her to get down on the floor, on Jon Teel's level, if necessary. She chose pale blue, a pleasing color that, in Julia's opinion, was calming. She looked through her perfume assortment for a scent that smelled of gardenia. Julia had long ago discovered that children have a high developed sense of smell; a pleasing scent was important. For good measure, she stuck her fingers in the melted wax of a cinnamon-scented candle on her kitchen counter and rubbed some on her wrists.

Julia presented herself at Carter Elementary School office armed with the order from Judge Green decreeing that Julia Hancock was to tutor the child Jon Teel as often as her schedule permitted, every day if necessary. Julia was not sure, but she believed that a court order superseded an order from the school board. The secretary rang for the principal, who soon appeared.

"Welcome to Carter Elementary, Mrs. Hancock. You come highly recommended. I am Ellen Jacoby, the principal here at Carter. We have received two different orders stating that you are to work with young Jon Teel as often as your schedule permits. The school board office and the juvenile court judge have both sent paperwork. You are doubly directed to take on what is developing into a difficult case. The young man is not reacting well to the classroom situation. His teacher is very good, but she has had little success in reaching him. She has fifteen other five-year-olds needing attention. We assigned an aide to Jon Teel for part of the day. She is not very well trained for children with special needs, I am afraid. She is with him in the library now. I will escort you there myself."

They walked down a long hallway and took a right turn into another hall. At the end of that passageway, they came to a door with a sign: library. The principal opened the door with a practiced hand, making no sound. They entered quietly. Julia considered herself to be a person in command of her emotions, but when she spotted the child in the back corner of the library, she nearly lost control. Her heart pounded. Tears welled up in her eyes. She cleared her throat and willed herself to remain calm. The principal gave her a knowing look. "I understand," she seemed to be saying.

The boy sat in a small chair with his head resting on his arms. A large woman was standing over him, haranguing him in a hoarse whisper.

"Child, you need to talk to us. You need to get yourself an education. You can't sit here all day and not open your mouth. How are you gonna learn? You gotta help us out."

The woman realized she had an audience. She stopped talking and turned to face Julia and the principal, not the least embarrassed.

"The child won't talk no matter what I do," she said, looking accusingly at the boy.

"That's fine, Mrs. Barne. You can go back to your regular classroom. Mrs. Hancock is here to work with Jon Teel."

Mrs. Barne gave Julia a look that said, "If you think you can do better than I can, you just try."

The principal bent down to Jon Teel and said, "This is Mrs. Hancock. She is here to help you. Do you remember Judge Green, Jon Teel? He sent Mrs. Julia to you."

With that, the principal turned on the heel of a sensible shoe and left the library. Julia breathed a silent, fervent prayer. She pulled out one of the small chairs and sat down on the side of the boy. She placed her hands on the table, palms outstretched, so that he could see them. Julia knew how to teach a child to read, but she had not ever had occasion to gain the trust of a child who had every reason to fear adults. She had to win him over somehow, to dip down into that pit of ruined childhood and pull out whatever remained. He had to be reached. He had to be saved. Julia had a sudden flash of insight that she could only ascribe to divine intervention. It was a voice that spoke to her heart, "What this child needs is unconditional, unremitting love. If you give him that, the rest will come."

"Jon Teel," she said, willing herself to speak softly and calmly, although she was anything but calm, "I am Julia. I am here to help you. I will never, never hurt you, I promise. I will care for you if you will let me. I have a lot of love to give, Jon Teel, and I will love you if you will let me."

Where did that come from, Julia wondered. Then she realized that it was the truth. She already did love this poor, battered child.

Thus, with baby steps, began the relationship of the wealthy widow Julia Hancock with the abandoned, abused child Jon Teel. Julia spent an hour with him that first day, hoping only to elicit a smile. Julia wanted some sort of an assessment, a baseline from which to begin, but she decided to throw the textbooks to the wind and use her natural instinct as a teacher and as a motherly woman—although not a mother.

She took the metal tray with the alphabet letters and spelled out her name, J-U-L-I-A. There was no response from the boy. Next, she spelled out his name, J-O-N T-E-E-L. Jon Teel responded.

"Jon Teel!" He pointed at the arranged letters and then at the center of his bony chest. Julia had to contain her brimming excitement at this first sign of response and at his recognition of the connection between the arranged letters and his name. This was a critical first step in the acquisition of language proficiency.

* * * * *

Julia returned to the school the next day and the day after that, and soon, she was spending most of her time with Jon Teel. This did not sit well with the members of her card-playing group. Every one of them had an opinion.

"Julia, you are going to make yourself sick over that boy and leave yourself open for a whole world of disappointment. There is no way this situation can have a happy outcome. Leave it to Auntie Jones and the people over at the school. They are the experts."

This was the pronouncement of Louella, known behind her back as the crepehanger. The old expression harkened back to Victorian days, when the homes of bereaved families were draped in black crepe fabric for the long mourning period. Louella could turn a child's birthday party into a wake with her dire predictions. Julia made polite noises but decided to turn a deaf ear. Her other friends were more difficult to ignore. They, too, thought Julia was devoting too much time and emotional energy to a case that was sure to have an unhappy outcome. The words of her oldest, dearest friend cut the deepest.

"Julia," Margot said, "you and I have been friends since before first grade. I tell you this in the name of our long-standing friendship. I believe you are transferring your unanswered need to be a mother onto this unfortunate child. In the end, it can only hurt you, and it will most certainly harm the child. You cannot—indeed no one in this world can—give this poor child what he needs or make up for what he has lost."

A surgeon's scalpel could not have cut more quickly or deeply. Upon hearing the words spoken by her dear friend, Julia had stood up immediately. Without saying a word, she left the room and the ongoing card game in midstream, while those well-intentioned but hurtful words hung in the air. She knew she could not trust her roiling emotions. She could only imagine how her friends must have dissected her reaction and her growing relationship with Jon Teel once she drove away.

Julia Digs In

Julia was not deterred. She continued to work with the boy and continued to be amazed by his innate intelligence. What concerned her was his lack of any ability to behave as a child. There was no joy, no playfulness. Julia tried everything she could think of, searching textbooks and even the Internet for ideas, but nothing worked. She brought in a variety of toys, but they seemed to hold no interest for Jon Teel. Auntie Jones reported the same sad behavior at her home. The only adjective Julia could think of to describe his behavior was "robotic."

The school environment was not conducive to the free play that Julia envisioned for Jon Teel. She decided to approach Auntie Jones first, and then the judge. She wanted to have Jon Teel come to her home, planning to enlist Florida's granddaughters, Orlie and Waveland, to engage the boy in structured play geared toward strengthening his social skills and his ability to trust.

"Julia," Auntie Jones declared, "if anyone can bring that boy out of his shell, you are the one. You have my unconditional permission and approval, and I will call Porteous Green if you need me to do it."

"Thanks, Auntie, but I will handle Porteous. I can't see how he would object."

*   *   *   *   *

Porteous gave his immediate approval, requesting only that the new plan go into effect the following week. He wanted to document the plan and get written approval from Ronnell Williams and her superiors at the Louisiana Department of Children and Family Services—DCFS.

"Julia," Porteous declared, "I think your idea is not only sound, but brilliant. Just allow me to fluff the feathers of the powers that be to keep everything on the up-and-up. Let's go with Tuesday. That way you can visit the school and tutor the boy Monday and work out the issue of transportation. I suspect Ronnell or another caseworker will have to drive him to your place unless we can get you approved as a driver."

The complications that never failed to arise with "the system" continued to amaze Julia. Nothing was simple.

*   *   *   *   *

True to his word, Porteous set the wheels in motion. By Tuesday, Ronnell appeared at the school ready to drive Jon Teel to Julia's home. She also had paperwork that, once completed, would allow Julia to drive Jon Teel to and from her home and also to and from Auntie Jones's home, as well as to medical and dental appointments. Ronnell jumped at the chance to implement Julia's help with her overloaded schedule.

*   *   *   *   *

Julia had come to respect the job the capable school principal did with the monumental task she had. The school had students from ages three in preschool to ten or eleven in fifth grade. Children barely out of diapers had to learn the rudiments of living in society in addition to reading, writing, and arithmetic during the hours they spent at school.

Julia decided to pay the principal a visit on her way to the library that Tuesday.

"I want to give you a big thank you, Mrs. Jacoby," Julia began. "I am so very impressed with the job you and your teachers are doing here. The little ones are babies, and somehow you are able to train them and teach them."

"I take that as high praise coming from you, Mrs. Hancock. Your reputation in education circles is well-known."

"Please, do call me Julia."

Julia explained her plan to take Jon Teel to her home each day. Instead of balking at the idea, the principal was instantly on board. The notion that Jon Teel could be in the sights of dangerous people had not escaped the principal.

"If you like, you could take him following his lunch in the cafeteria and have him for the entire afternoon. That way, his formal lesson could be given at your home followed by his playtime. Then you could return him directly to his foster home."

It was more than Julia had hoped for, and she began immediately. Reading was the key that would unlock many doors, including clues to Jon Teel's obscure past. Julia felt that, with structured guidance and one-on-one teaching, he could soon be reading. She began with the sight words on the basic list. His quick mastery astounded Julia.

The Dolch Basic Primer sight words were an old standby for Julia. She expected to spend several weeks helping Jon Teel gain mastery of the list. Such words as *all*, *at*, *came*, *did*, *do*, and *eat* had to be recognized and memorized on sight, not by sounding them out phonetically. Julia was blown away when Jon Teel knew the first ten words after they had been presented to him once.

"Jon," Julia might begin, "what do I mean when I ask if you ate *all* your breakfast?"

"You mean I didn't leave nothing on my plate."

"Exactly, Jon. You didn't leave anything on your plate. You ate it *all*."

And so it continued. The quick retention and mastery on the part of the boy spurred Julia on to challenge him more, and he flourished under her obvious approval. He learned to recognize, pronounce, and write one hundred basic sight words and soon was sounding out an amazing range of words and sentences.

Julia and Jon worked each day on the language skills until Orlie and Waveland came bursting in after their school day ended. Julia put them in charge of "play and numbers." Florida's granddaughters were irrepressibly happy, enthusiastic children.

"Just what the doctor ordered," Julia thought. Perfect for bringing the boy out of his shell.

*   *   *   *   *

One morning, the sheriff telephoned.

"Julia," Joe Blanchard began, "Doc Christian and I have just conferred with Porteous Green. We want to have a visit with your boy. Rather than bother Auntie Jones, we thought we might come by your place to see how he is faring."

Julia's heart gave a little jolt. She felt certain three grown men would threaten Jon, even though he had met all of them. He had had several follow-up appointments with the doctor, who was pleased with his progress.

"Joe, give me a day to set it up. I want you to be here on Thursday when I arrive with Jon Teel. I can tell him you came for lunch. In fact, *do* come for lunch. Florida and I will have something ready for you."

Julia prepared Jon Teel on the drive from the school telling him that his "friends" the judge, the sheriff, and the doctor had come for lunch and decided to wait to tell him hello. Instead of shutting down as Julia anticipated, the boy agreed.

"They are my first friends here," Jon Teel said, "except for Auntie Jones. You came next, Julia." Julia's heart fairly sang at this proof of progress. A constant barrage of love and positivity really could begin to undo years of damage.

The visit was brief but enough to assure the three men that the boy had made astounding progress. Orlie and Waveland had practiced shaking hands with Jon Teel in a game they called "young gentleman." Julia told Jon Teel to show the men "young gentleman." He made the round of all three men, giving a slight bow and shaking each man's hand in turn. The three men were flabbergasted. In a few short weeks, the boy had blossomed.

Judge Green was particularly pleased, because this meant one less load on Auntie Jones's aging shoulders.

"Julia, help her however you can. She will never quit, but I know she needs to slow down," Porteous said as he left Julia's sunporch that day.

An Untimely Death

Then the unthinkable happened as the judge's words turned into a fore-warning. Julia received the news directly from Judge Green in an early morning phone call. She could hear the tears in his voice.

"Julia, tragedy has struck our community. The most unfortunate of our young children have suffered an incalculable loss. Auntie Jones died in her bed in the night, and I am afraid it was our young Jon Teel who found her. The girl who comes in to help in the morning found him lying next to her in the bed. No tears. No response. I am not a psychologist, but I would call his state catatonic. I hope this doesn't undo all the progress you have made with the child. I could really use your help here. Could you take the boy to Auntie's funeral? I think it is crucially important that he attends. He needs the closure, and he needs to know that he still has somebody who cares for him. He has been placed with another foster family temporarily. I will send you the address and the funeral arrangements."

Julia readily agreed, wishing she could simply go and pick up Jon Teel immediately. She decided the best course was to follow the plan laid out by the judge and pick Jon Teel up in time for the funeral.

* * * * *

After the sad funeral of Auntie Jones, Jon Teel had reluctantly left Julia's side and gone off with Ronnell Williams, the social worker assigned to the boy's case. Julia liked Ronnell when they had worked CASA cases together, and she admired her even more as they worked together to help

Jon Teel. Julia found Ronnell to be fair, committed, and unsentimental, all qualities that Julia considered essential to the job of dealing with the sad, broken lives of neglected and abused children. Jon Teel was staying in the assigned temporary foster home where, according to a whispered report from Ronnell, the boy was not doing well.

*   *   *   *   *

Julia drove back into town after the funeral, going immediately to the courthouse to answer the summons of Judge Porteous Green, which had been passed along to her after the service. "The wisdom of Solomon," her husband had often said of Judge Green's rulings. Today, Julia found him in his chambers, still wiping funeral perspiration from his face with a pristine handkerchief. The cemetery had been brutally hot, taking a toll on both the judge and Julia.

"Julia," the judge began, "neither one of us has the time or the patience for tiptoeing around and talking about the weather. I am gravely concerned about young Jon Teel. The child has suffered more physical and emotional pain in his short life than most of us experience in a life-time. Your training and your natural instincts have worked wonders with him in the brief time you have spent with him over at the elementary school and in your home. I cannot bear the thought of that progress being undone. Now that Auntie Jones, God rest her gentle soul, has gone to her reward, I want you to consider taking Jon Teel in as a foster child. Before you bring up your age or other requirements for foster parenting, let me say that I am the juvenile court judge for this district and I have wide latitude. I can rule and overrule. Age will not be a problem. Your extensive CASA training and experience can guarantee temporary certification until you can complete the home study requirements. I don't want an answer today. I want you to sleep on it. But just know that the new foster mother is reporting that the child has completely shut down since Auntie's death. We hold out little hope for locating the birth parents because we do not believe that Teel is his surname but rather some sort of nickname. Still, for the sake of due diligence, we have run combinations of the name through local and national databases, which resulted in dead ends. We have no leads other than the suspicions of the Harris County sheriff over in Texas. I have begun the TPR process—termination of parental rights—on the strength of the verified severe physical abuse of the child. I want to get that ball rolling."

Julia sat for a few moments in stunned silence. In truth, she had thought about requesting to take the child in but put the thought aside because she did not think it would be allowed due to her age. Now the offer was being made by the man with the power to make it happen. It was too much to take in after the wrenching funeral service and Jon Teel's clinging to her in such helpless, hopeless despair. Agreeing to think it over and give an answer on Monday, Julia left the courthouse and went home.

After a restless, dream-filled night, Julia sat in her sunny back room. This was her favorite room in the huge house. The morning sun streamed in at an angle from the east, casting a warm glow over the bayou and bathing the room in light. Julia had her coffee and light breakfast and read her prayers and daily meditation. Before opening the newspaper, she performed her other daily ritual, pulling a strip of paper from the wooden box of wise sayings. Generally, Julia chose the wise saying of the day with little thought; it was a daily habit. Today, she put her elbows on the table, rubbed her temples, and prayed fervently.

"God, Jesus, I really need a sign. My heart tells me to take this child in and love him. My head tells me this is the craziest thing I have ever considered. I am sixty-five years old, my life is steady and secure, and this would be the biggest gamble on the unknown that I could ever take. But Porteous thinks I can do it, and Abbot Joseph continues to tell me that my work in this life is not done, that I still have much to do. Let the paper I choose for today be my sign."

She reached into the wooden box, shuffled the papers around as though she were choosing a winning lottery ticket, and pulled out a crumpled strip. It was on the tissue-thin blue letter paper favored by her grandmother. In a fine old-fashioned script, in faded blue ink, her grandmother Ethel had written, "Whatsoever you do for the least of my brethren, that you do unto me."

Abbot Joseph

Julia had promised Judge Green that she would give him an answer by the time he got to the courthouse on Monday morning. As she sipped her coffee, she reached once more into her mother's box of wise sayings. This one read, "*Turn to God for help when making big decisions.*" Her scheduled visit with her confessor, Abbot Joseph at the Abbey north of Covington, was not for two weeks, but Julia felt the need for the cool unbiased sounding board that Abbot Joseph provided. He would not give an opinion, but he had an uncanny way of asking questions in such a manner that, by the end of the session, Julia knew she would have her answer. She set up the appointment.

She backed her silver Lexus out of the garage, set the sound system to play her six favorite CDs, and headed for New Orleans. She had met the monk when she went with a group of ladies from the parish on a daylong retreat at the abbey. Abbot Joseph gave one part of the retreat, then offered confession for any who might feel the need. Julia went to his cubicle of an office where they chatted, he gave her absolution, and she made an appointment for the same time the next month. This had been going on for twelve years, and Julia had never felt better spiritually. She had not slept well since the judge had thrown out the idea that she take Jon Teel into her home as a foster child, but now that she was on the way to see the abbot, the uneasy feelings lifted. She would have an answer soon; she knew it.

"Julia, you know it is my habit to ask that you weigh all the reasons for and against anything life-changing that you propose to do," the portly little monk asserted shortly after she arrived, "so let's begin with the obvious. Do you have the room to house the boy and the finances to feed and clothe and educate him?"

Julia started to protest because she was certain that Abbot Joseph knew the answers to these questions. Besides, the state would provide foster care funds. Julia had decided not to request the funds as she had no need for financial assistance.

"Yes, I have plenty of room and more than enough money."

"So the issue is whether or not you are physically and mentally prepared for the challenge of rearing the child. How is your health?"

"Good. In fact, practically perfect."

"If you don't mind my asking, how old are you?"

"I don't mind. I am sixty-five."

"So let's say you take the child. If you keep him for twelve years, until he is seventeen or eighteen, you will be eighty-two. But remember, sixty is the new forty," he chuckled.

"Yes, and I know you tell me every time I come for confession that God is not finished with me and my work on Earth is not nearly done."

"Oh, did I say that?" He asked the question with feigned innocence.

"My worry is that I do not want to take the child in only to try and fail. He has been abused and thrown away and experienced loss too many times in his short life."

"My dear Julia, you have the answer already. You are drawn to this child. He has awakened in you a motherly instinct that is obvious to any who know you. What about your circle of close friends? Are they supportive?"

Abbot Joseph probably knew the answer to this question as well. He would have made a good lawyer.

"Most of them are not very supportive. They think I should be enjoying my retirement years. They think I'm crazy. But mainly I think they don't want to lose a faithful gin player."

"My final question is this: Are you feeling fulfilled these days? As though you have done sufficient meaningful work in your life?"

Julia mulled this over for a full minute.

"The honest-to-God answer is no. I feel as though I have more to give."

"Well, then, what is your next step?"

"I'll see the judge Monday morning, and then I will pick up Jon Teel at his foster home. But first, I have to get Florida on board, and that will be no easy task. I can't do it without her."

"I have one more thing to add, Julia," Abbot Joseph said. "Do not think for one minute that this is going to be easy. You will need all the resources at your disposal and then some. You will need to dig deep for wellsprings of faith and strength you do not realize you have. But you do have them, and you will find them, and you will do this. I know it with every fiber of my faith and my considerable intuition into the hearts of humankind."

Florida and Her Girls

Florida Johnson was one of those rare individuals who seldom has a bad day. She sang, she whistled, and she talked to herself, asking rhetorical questions and then answering them. Although she was a faithful old-school Catholic, she had a whole repertoire of Protestant hymns. Some were the old Negro spirituals from decades past, but others were what Julia thought of as Baptist hymns. One was a particular favorite of Julia's, although she did not dare mention it to Florida for fear that she would be too embarrassed to sing it again. It included the refrain, "And man took a tree, an innocent tree, and made a cross for him." This image of the tree, something so beautiful, turned into an instrument of torture and death, struck a chord in Julia's heart.

Florida had grown up with Julia, an equal in the household. Many times, it was Florida's voice of reason that kept Julia out of trouble with her very proper parents and her doubly old-school grandmother. Florida and Julia's mother both spoke more cultured and grammatically correct English than Julia did and prided themselves on knowing the intricacies of southern etiquette. Florida could set a table for a formal five-course dinner better than any blue-blooded lady in town and took great pride in keeping Julia on the straight and narrow regarding the rules of decorum. They often butted heads over Julia's growing propensity for pantsuits as opposed to proper dresses, particularly for Mass. But, all in all, their relationship was one based on mutual love and respect, made even more agreeable by the fact that voices raised in anger had seldom been heard in the rooms or on the grounds of Dapplefield. With a lineage of intelligent and articulate judges as de facto lords of the manor, daily affairs of the great house had been conducted with quiet good sense, respect, and dignity for well over a hundred years.

Florida had attended the public schools of Bakerville, while Julia attended the parochial schools. A self-motivated student, Florida had excelled. She attended the college courses offered in Bakerville by the university in Lafayette, then she commuted to finish her degree in business and finance. The Chandler family would have underwritten her education, but it was important to Florida that she finance her own education. She would be beholden to no one for her hard-won degree. She held her own as a nineteen-year-old in the intimidating presence of Julia's father, Judge Chandler, behind his massive desk in his study.

"Florida, child, I don't understand why you persist in this recalcitrant behavior. I want to finance your college education just as I will finance that of my own daughter Julia."

"Sir, I am no longer a child, and I appreciate your generosity. It is important to me to pay my own way. I can do it, and I *will* do it." And do it she did. She got a job in a bank in Lafayette, where she worked until she married and moved back to Bakerville. Judge Chandler persuaded her that it would be a personal favor to him if she could see her way clear to come to work for him and learn the workings of the family business. Sugarcane land, rental properties, and oil leases—there was enough for a full-time manager.

There was whispered talk in Bakerville about how in the world the judge could trust a young black girl with his business, but, in his usual blunt fashion, the judge shut them down by pronouncing loudly and proudly at a meeting of the local Rotary Club that he had "the best damn manager in St. Mary Parish."

It was Florida's proven ability with numbers and balance sheets that prompted John Hancock to offer her to continue in the job upon the death of the retired judge. He offered Florida a position he labeled "manager of the estate," which she readily accepted. Julia could not have made it through John's death without Flo. She understood all the intricacies of their properties, both those inherited from Julia's parents and grandparents and those acquired by John. The settling of the estate went smoothly, facilitated by the self-effacing Florida Johnson. Widowed at a young age herself, Florida understood the challenges Julia faced.

Florida had for some time been the surrogate mother to her two granddaughters. Their mother, Jacqueline, Florida's only child, had shown great promise. She graduated valedictorian of her class, but love got in the way of her college scholarship dreams. She married her high school sweetheart, vowing to finish her education. Their two baby girls, born a year apart, slowed Jackie down, but she and her young husband worked day jobs and commuted to Lafayette for night courses at UL. A grinding collision with an oil tanker stopped at a train track ended all their dreams and gave grandmother Florida two baby girls to rear. After a difficult period of mourning, Florida jumped into her dual role as mother and grandmother with both feet.

Florida had been well taken care of upon the death of Julia's husband John. Julia's father had already given Florida the tidy brick home on Third Street that had belonged to his mother, knowing that his only daughter Julia would inherit the big house, Dapplefield Manor. Letting Julia know that the bequests were not charity but rather were Florida's earned right, John had left Florida a generous sum of money and, in addition, had set up trusts for the education of Florida's two granddaughters, Orlando and Waveland, named by their dead father for the places where he and their mother had vacationed. Before his untimely death, Florida had come to love and respect her young son-in-law in spite of the fact that she did not approve of their marrying so young.

Julia always felt that she had been left out of crucial family discussions between her father and her husband John. After her father's death, there were times when she felt that John and Florida had some sort of conspiratorial connection. If this were the case, Julia would never ask or pry; she assumed if they were leaving her out, it must be for her own good. But it was difficult to contain her curiosity.

On one occasion, after Florida and John had been closeted in John's study for over an hour, Julia found herself fuming. She decided to confront one of them, knowing she was no match for the two of them together. She decided she would tackle Florida.

"Flo," she began, after John had departed for his office, "it really bothers me that you and John have so much to talk about, and you seem bound and determined to leave me out of the business."

Julia expected Florida to take offense and become argumentative. Her reaction stopped Julia in her tracks.

"Julia, I am sure that if you really are interested in whether we ask three-eighths or a quarter on an oil lease and whether we agree to one-sixth instead of one-fifth on a poor farmer who is going broke, John will be happy to include you. If I were you, though, I would appreciate a good husband who wants to spare you all those humdrum details and allow you to focus on your demanding schedule of teaching at the university."

Julia decided to accept Florida's sensible answer and didn't worry about it again.

After that exchange, it was an accepted though unspoken agreement that Florida would continue to manage Dapplefield as long as her health allowed. She was adept at the finances and figures and a great help in running the house. Besides, there was nowhere else Florida would rather be. They shared the mundane tasks and had Mrs. Tee to come in several days a week to help with the cleaning and laundry.

* * * * *

Florida had strong feelings about Julia's involvement with the mystery child. Florida did not welcome change. She liked things on an even keel, and the boy had three strikes against him. First, his family background was unknown. As far as Florida was concerned, knowing one's family history was important. Florida herself would not want to tackle the job of rearing such a child. Second, he was severely abused, which brought on another whole set of problems. Finally, with unknown parents out there who had probably hurt him in the first place, there was no telling what might happen. They could arrive in the night with guns blazing.

* * * * *

When Julia's Lexus came rolling up the driveway from her visit with Abbot Joseph, Florida was waiting at the door, armed and ready with her sensible arguments.

"Julia, I can tell by the set of your jaw that you have decided to do what the judge wants and take the child in."

Florida started in before Julia had time to set her purse down. She had stopped at a farmer's market on Highway 90 in Des Allemands, thinking that an array of fresh vegetables might distract Florida. Julia had anticipated correctly that Florida would be anti-Jon Teel, and it was crucial that she win her over if this fostering project had any chance of succeeding. Before she spoke, she arranged the tomatoes and green beans she had bought in a wooden bowl on the counter.

"Flo," Julia began, "I love you like a sister, and I value your opinion. I know what you are going to say. Taking in any abused child would be hard enough, but a child whose background is so very different from my own makes it even harder. He has been severely mistreated and abused, and God only knows what kind of sorry psychotic excuse for a human being did this to him. Our lives here are good, simple, and on a safe path. I am sixty-five years old, and you are even older. All of that is true. But Flo, God help me, I want to do this, and I can't do it without you. I can't do it without you and your precious girls. It won't be a permanent adoption. It will be a foster placement under the supervision of Judge Green's court. The sheriff knows the whole situation and will be monitoring things to keep us safe."

Then Julia brought out the heavy artillery. Florida was a serious student of the Bible and used it as her guide for daily living.

"Do you know what I pulled out of the saying box before I left for the Abbey? 'Whatsoever you do for the least of my brethren, you do for me.' If that poor little boy isn't the least of the least brethren, I don't know where we can look to find him."

Florida sat down slowly at the kitchen table.

"Julia, you know I hate it when you go all Christian on me, and I know you are right, and I feel like a selfish, self-righteous Pharisee. Let's give the boy a week and see how we do with him. You know the girls will mother him to death if we let them."

Julia never dreamed it might be that easy. Florida had caved much more quickly than she anticipated. And so the die was cast.

Jumping through Hoops

Julia attended Mass with Florida and the girls the following Sunday. First, they had breakfast together while Florida and Julia announced the impending arrival of Jon Teel. Then, with great fanfare, they picked a paper from the box of wise sayings. The girls loved the tradition. It was Waveland's turn to choose. She stuck her small brown hand into the box, closed her eyes, and said, "Oh, please, God, let it be a good one!" She pulled out a paper written on what appeared to be legal pad paper and read, "We must stand up for the rights of those treated unjustly because we see Jesus in them." Julia's heart pounded. That sounded like something her father would have seen fit to add to the box. It echoed Julia's sentiments about Jon Teel exactly. The four of them agreed that the wise saying was perfect for what was to come into their lives. They walked over to the church together, discussing the coming of Jon Teel on the way.

"Girls," Julia said, "we are really going to need your help with the boy. You cannot even imagine how he has been abused. You will need to be gentle with him, and not be put off if he doesn't act like you expect him to. The poor child doesn't even know how to play."

The two girls were fifth and seventh graders who considered themselves very mature and grown up. They immediately jumped on the Jon Teel bandwagon.

"Oh, Miss Julia, we are going to help. Whatever you need, you just tell us. Our friends will help, too!" This was from Orlando—Orlie—the older of the two.

"Well, girls, for the time being, the judge and the sheriff do not want us to talk about Jon Teel living with us. We don't know who hurt him, and we don't want to take any chances."

Julia was afraid this might frighten the girls or put them off, but instead, they were thrilled with the intrigue and excitement.

"We can keep a secret, Miss Julia, but we were hoping he might come to St. John," Waveland said.

"For the time being, I will homeschool him, but I will depend on you two girls to come in and help me with play time. He doesn't even seem to know what to do with a toy."

That threw the girls into a frenzy of excited talk about how to play with the child and how impossible it seemed that a child would not know what to do with a toy in the first place. They vowed to pray hard at Mass that Jon Teel would be happy with them and that his scarred little spirit could be healed.

*   *   *   *   *

The first thing Monday morning, Julia drove to the courthouse to be there when the doors opened. She did not wait to call for an appointment, because she knew this was a week when court was in session. She also knew Porteous would be waiting to hear from her, and her best possibility for seeing him would be to present herself in person when he arrived at his chambers. She was correct; in fact, Julia and the judge found themselves sharing an elevator on the way up. They said nothing other than exchanging morning pleasantries in the crowded elevator on the way up to the courtroom floor. Both knew their conversation must be held in strict confidence.

Judge Green stowed his bulky leather satchel under his desk and offered Julia coffee. Lulu, his clerk of many years, bustled about with an air of importance, coming in with stacks of official documents as though reminding them that this was a work day and the wheels of justice needed to get oiled and turning.

The judge was not perturbed.

"Lulu, Mrs. Hancock and I have business pertaining to an ongoing case. We will need a few minutes of privacy, so I would appreciate it if you would take all of today's documents out to the courtroom and stack them in order with today's docket. Also, announce that I am dealing with an emergency situation regarding an ongoing case and court should convene in thirty minutes or less. Anyone on this morning's docket should not leave the premises."

Lulu nodded, picked up the stack of legal-sized documents, and left the judge's chambers, closing the heavy door quietly behind her.

"Julia, have you reached a decision?"

"Yes. I'll take Jon Teel in as a foster child for as long as I am able to help him."

The judge breathed an audible sigh of relief.

"Julia, you have made me a happy man in a generally unhappy profession. Now, I must tell you that I intend for this case to be handled with the utmost strictness in adhering to the letter of the law. There are elements to the case that could complicate things, and there is a remote but real cause to believe that the boy—and even you—might be in physical danger at some point."

If Judge Green expected a reaction from Julia, he was disappointed. She sat in silence, waiting for him to continue.

"First things first. I want you certified as a foster parent. That won't be hard. We waive the training requirement on a regular basis, especially in emergencies for family members such as grandparents, and because there is such a shortage of suitable foster parents. Plus, there is the fact that you have been working with and making progress with the boy. I think we are good on all the qualifications. Your home will have to be inspected. You will have to be fingerprinted and checked for criminal background—all the usual things. You have smoke detectors and fire extinguishers, don't you? You will breeze through, but all of these things have to be done before we put the boy in your care. I am going to call down to the sheriff and tell him I am sending you down the back elevator for fingerprints. Then I am going to call Ronnell and tell her to drop everything and get someone over to your house this morning to do the inspection. You will have to show them your entire house and show them where you intend for the child to sleep and so forth. Show them your fire extinguishers. Hell, I'll get the fire chief over there. He designed the system for you, didn't he? I'll get the sheriff on the criminal background check, and I will get back to you if I have forgotten anything. But Julia, I cannot emphasize enough that I have heard some disturbing things out of the sheriff's office in Harris County, Texas. They are playing it close to the vest because it ties in with an ongoing undercover drug operation that they have a lot riding on. There was word of a child involved, and that child has not been seen. If—and it is a big if—it ties back to Jon Teel, I will be informed, and you will be in the loop."

Julia had not spoken a word through the judge's long explanation of procedure. Now one thought came into her mind.

"Judge, with your permission, I would like to enlist the help of Jamal."

J-Max

Jamal Maximo Jackson, a.k.a. J-Max Jackson of NFL fame, was a protégé and dear friend of Julia's. Weighing in at 295 pounds, he was trim and muscular. His six feet five frame carried the weight well. He was an imposing figure. J-Max was still Jamal when he and Julia had crossed paths many years ago. Jack Coltrane, coach of the football team at the local Catholic high school, had called Julia frantically in midsummer.

"Mrs. Hancock, I am told that you are a reading magician. I have a kid over here who has all kinds of potential. His only trouble is he cannot read. Not a word. Because of his size and his attitude, teachers and principals in the public schools over in Forester gave him social promotions to get rid of him. I think he can learn if you can maybe use some of your tricks. You may be his only chance."

Julia's husband John had recently retired, and they had been making travel plans. Throughout the coach's plea, she had been telling herself, "No, no, do not get involved." When he said that Julia might be the boy's only chance, she relented and found herself agreeing to go over to the school that afternoon with some testing materials and see what she could diagnose.

When Julia arrived, she found Jamal Maximo Jackson sitting in a regular classroom desk that was too small for his huge size. His sullen expression did not put Julia off. She had dealt with obstinacy before. She also had a flash of insight about the coach's interest. This young man would be an asset to any football team by simply setting foot on the field. His very size was intimidating.

In working with high school faculties, Julia had at first been critical of the emphasis on sports. Through the years, though, she had come to realize the powerful positive influence a good athletic coach could have on failing students, particularly the male ones. They would study and succeed for a coach when they had failed for years for lack of trying. Sports were a powerful incentive for many students.

Julia introduced herself to Jamal and had him come with her to the empty cafeteria. There she spread her materials out on a large table with chairs that better accommodated his size. Within fifteen minutes, Julia realized that Jamal was severely dyslexic. She could not believe that this had gone undiagnosed through eight years of public education. He had been living with his mother, who had given up and sent him to Bakerville to live with a grandmother. Julia knew the woman. She was a devout Catholic and probably the reason Jamal found himself at the Catholic school. Jamal's grandmother would sacrifice anything for her grandson's education. If money should prove to be an issue, Julia was certain the coach would secure an athletic scholarship for his potential new star.

"Jamal," she began after completing the tests, "you can learn to read, and I can help you. You are a smart guy. If you will work with me, you will be reading by the time school starts. What I will need for you to do is come to my house for tutoring. I have all my reading materials there. It is not far from the school. Come to my house each morning when you finish your football practice."

"What about the cost?" Jamal asked. "My Gramaw don't have a lot of extra money."

"Jamal, you would be doing me a twofold favor by allowing me to do this. I will count it as a contribution to the school that educated me, and I will keep alive the skills I learned in a very expensive education. You will make me feel useful. But you will have to put in the work."

"I ain't lazy, Miz Julia. My teachers think I am, but I ain't."

After this exchange, Jamal seemed to perk up a bit and agreed to come to Julia's home the next day. When Julia answered the front door, she found Jamal looking a bit abashed by the grandeur of the fine old home. John came out of his study and shook Jamal's hand, a gesture that seemed unfamiliar to the young man.

"Welcome to our home, Jamal. It is very good to meet you," John said.

"Jamal, this is my husband, Judge Hancock," Julia said. "Come this way. We will work in the sunroom."

Thus began a summer of the hardest work Julia had ever put in with a student. Once Jamal realized that he could decipher letters and then words and finally sentences, it was as though a curtain lifted. Through the long weeks of summer, the sullen boy blossomed into a confident young man. John came in to join in their discussions about stories, and Jamal began to pick up the nuances of standard English conversation. Soon, he was staying for lunch with the Hancocks. Julia and John together taught him the intricacies of proper dining etiquette. Jamal was not one of the typical, sullen teenagers with an attitude. He truly thirsted for knowledge and was innately intelligent. His learning disability had both frustrated him and held him back from any sort of progress. *Thank God for a grandmother who would not give up on her grandson*, Julia mused as she marveled at the young man's progress.

During that summer, Jamal learned to be a young gentleman. The skills of reading, manners, conversation, polite discussion, and arguing a point served him well in his high school education and in his later college and pro football careers. Jamal finished in the top ten in his high school class. He went to LSU on a football scholarship where he played offensive lineman. His brilliant blocking helped LSU win the national championship. It was at LSU that Jamal became J-Max. He went on to earn two Super Bowl rings, one with the New England Patriots and one with the much-beloved New Orleans Saints.

J-Max Jackson was the nearest thing to a saint that the town of Bakerville had produced.

Upon his retirement from pro football, he became a popular football commentator. His clear speech, easy demeanor, quick wit, and off-the-cuff literary references gained him fans across America. Julia was not a football fan, but she had followed his career avidly. It warmed her heart now to hear Jamal utter phrases that came directly from her now-departed husband. John, until his death, thought of Jamal as the son he never had and shared Julia's pride in his success.

Jamal spent the off-season in Bakerville with his frail grandmother. He had built her a large, comfortable home with a tall wrought-iron fence equipped with an automatic gate and a secure alarm system. He did not want his grandmother bothered by overly excited fans. She still considered J-Max to be her precious little Jamal.

J-Max's favorite activity while he was in residence in Bakerville was donning his uniform as an official but unpaid sheriff's deputy. His uniform included all the recognizable tools of the trade with the exception of a gun. He had handcuffs, a loud whistle, pepper spray, and a long, slender black metal baton that the local children swore had magical properties. The baton was sixteen inches in length, beautifully crafted in Germany. With the press of a tiny hidden button, a spring-loaded mechanism sent the tip of it out, instantly extending it to five feet. With this magic wand, he could tickle a child or swat a misbehaving teenager, all the while entertaining his adoring fans.

J-Max loved patrolling events attended by young people. His imposing, easily recognized figure assured good behavior. The sheriff called on him often, as did Judge Green. He could reach recalcitrant teenagers who arrived in Judge Green's courtroom at a crossroads. They could go down the sewer, succumbing to a life of drugs and crime, or they could be saved. Jamal had been where they were, and he was a living proof that there was a better way, and that education was the key that opened the door.

Julia loved Jamal like the son she never had, and he felt the same about Julia. Much to Julia's embarrassment, he had given her credit for his success in more than one nationally televised interview. He was a frequent visitor to her home when he was in residence in Bakerville.

When Julia returned home from the courthouse and her meeting with the judge, she telephoned Jamal to apprise him of her intention to foster Jon Teel and invited Jamal to come to meet Jon Teel once she had him living in her home. She felt that a strong, positive male influence would be invaluable in the rehabilitation of Jon Teel.

"And Jamal," she added, "you must approach the child with great care. He has been horribly abused, and we have to try in every way not to frighten him. The truth of the matter is, because of what has happened to him and the people we believe to be involved, we may all need protection at some point, and I know I can count on you."

Jamal, J-Max, readily agreed to follow Julia's lead when the time came.

More Hoops

As Julia finished the call to Jamal, the front doorbell chimed. Telling Florida she would answer it, Julia went to the door to find Ronnell and her supervisor, Hannah Clarkson, on the front gallery, briefcases in hand. They were all business, and Julia appreciated their professionalism. For her part, Julia called Florida in to be a part of the proceedings. In fact, it had occurred to Julia that it might be a good idea to have Florida as a witness and also to perhaps have her certified as a foster parent. She would see how things went today before she floated the idea by Flo.

Julia invited them into the front hall, and then directed them to the formal living room just off the hall. It was a lovely room, decorated at great expense by Julia's mother, but it proved the old adage that one got what one paid for. It was as pristine and attractive today as it had been fifty years ago.

Good taste stands the test of time was Julia's fleeting thought before getting down to the business at hand.

"Can I offer you ladies coffee or tea before we begin?" Julia asked.

Hannah Clarkson declined for the two of them and began.

"We are here at the direction of Judge Porteous Green of the Sixteenth Judicial Court to conduct an interview of Julia Chandler Hancock and an inspection of these premises prior to the possible placement of a foster child into your care here in this residence."

Julia noted with surprise that Ronnell was videotaping the proceedings.

Hannah stopped and said, "Mrs. Hancock, I neglected to ask your permission to video what we do here today. Judge Green is a stickler for the law, and I assure you this is for your legal protection as well as for verification for legal purposes."

Julia readily agreed, but she knew that in all her dealings with CASA and the juvenile court, she had never heard of such meticulous record-keeping. It was as though Porteous knew there would be legal troubles down the road.

The interview and inspection went off without a hitch, the video camera recording every word and panning every room in the house, including the upstairs bedroom next to her own that Julia had earmarked for Jon Teel. Instead of the tall canopy beds in most of the other bedrooms, this room had two twin beds with turned Jenny Lind spindles. It had been Julia's when she was a child, but in later years, it had been transformed into a guest room. It was simply furnished, light and airy, and thoroughly attractive. The two child welfare specialists representing the Department of Children and Family Services made no comments whatsoever. They did not so much as raise an eyebrow in approval or disapproval. They made it clear that they were there to question, record, and report but to give no opinions or answers. Julia understood and asked nothing of them. Julia could tell that Florida was using every ounce of her willpower to contain herself and hold her tongue. Julia knew that Florida found them brazen and pushy, two qualities Flo could not abide. Julia would have to explain it all later. She had not even had time to catch Flo up on the meeting with Judge Green, and she was still trying to decide how much to tell Flo and what—if anything—to withhold.

The last bit of the puzzle was the fire safety inspection. The fire chief himself came by to demonstrate to the two DCFS workers how the system worked, with smoke and carbon monoxide sensors hardwired into the house and a sprinkler system built in as well. There was at least one fire extinguisher in each room.

"Overkill," the fire chief pronounced, "but effective and definitely good to go."

Jon Teel Comes Home

The next morning as Julia sat in the sunroom reading her wise saying of the day—"Think well. Speak well. Do well."—there was a tap at the back door and Julia saw the smiling face of Porteous Green. She jumped up to let him in, poured him a cup of coffee, and showed him her wise saying of the morning. On an impulse, she went to the buffet and brought the old box to the breakfast room table.

"Before you tell me the verdict of yesterday's proceedings, pick another paper from the box. That one I chose is totally uninspiring. In fact, I may throw it out."

This was an idle threat. She could never bring herself to throw away any of the sayings that her progenitors thought worthy of remembering.

Porteous played along. Julia knew from his beaming expression that the news was good.

"Well, now, just look at that one. If that doesn't just beat all and put the icing on the cake, I don't know what does. Here, Julia. You do the honors."

Julia read the yellowed paper in a shaky voice: "This day I asked my Julia to marry me. I never want us to look back on our lives and regret that fear cheated us out any of the best things in life."

"Julia, if that isn't a good omen, I do not know what is. The DCFS ladies passed you with flying colors. Naturally, your criminal background check was totally good. The fact that you do not have a fenced backyard is not a problem because your property is so large. Just a suggestion, but you may want to consider putting up a tall board fence somewhere on the back side where the boy can play outdoors without prying eyes. Otherwise, all is set, and Ronnell can bring him today if you are ready."

"Porteous, I don't think I have ever been so ready but at the same time so unready for anything in my life. But I have loved that child since I set eyes on him on television getting in that big police cruiser in Lafayette, and I want to give this the very best I have got."

"Well, then, let me call Ronnell and set the wheels in motion. The one other thing we have not discussed is security. Have you spoken with J-Max?"

"I have, and he is totally on board. Of course, he is away working a good deal of the time, especially during football season, but he will certainly do what he can."

"How about your husband's right-hand man? You know, the fellow he hired as a bodyguard when he defended the young man everyone thought killed the Spiller girl?"

That had been a horrible time in their lives. John had believed in the young man's innocence, and a last-minute confession from the real murderer had proven him correct, but he had had death threats during the trial and had hired the services of a fellow who knew his way around criminals and could use a gun if the need arose. He had been a marine and then a guard at Angola, but Julia thought he might be working off-shore. It was worth a try. What had Porteous so concerned about their safety?

As though reading her mind, he said, "Julia, are we alone?"

"Yes, Porteous, totally. Florida has gone over to the school for Orlie's teacher conference. What is going on?"

"This has to remain between the two of us. Do not even tell Florida. Nothing may come of it. The body of a young Hispanic woman was pulled from the bay just off San Jacinto State Park near Houston last week. It was badly decomposed, but the coroner has ruled it a homicide with similarities to killings carried out by a Mexican drug cartel making major inroads into South Texas. They were able to match DNA to a young woman who showed up at an emergency room in Beaumont a few months back with a broken arm and other injuries, obviously from a beating. Julia, one of her injuries was a missing pinkie finger, an old injury that had not gotten medical attention. The ER doctor planned to keep her overnight, but she disappeared on them. Julia, this was two days after Jon Teel showed up at the bus station in Lafayette." Porteous paused, drew a long breath, and wiped his forehead with a clean white handkerchief.

"What is happening as we speak is that a representative of the coroner's office in Houston is on his way here now in an unmarked vehicle with a sample of that woman's DNA. We have DNA from Jon Teel already on file from Dr. Christian's examination. This could be the big break we are looking for, but it could put the boy in mortal danger. The Houston sheriff is so concerned about a leak that he does not want anyone in his department to know what is going on. The guy bringing the sample has no idea what he is carrying. This could be as big and bad as it gets in law enforcement. Are you still in?"

Julia wiped a bead of perspiration from her upper lip with a paper napkin. She looked up at the gently whirling ceiling fan and then back at Porteous Green.

"Yes, Porteous, I am in. Let's show that boy some love and mercy and bring him back to life. And remind me to show you the excellent hidden safe room my grandfather put in when the bootleggers were after him during Prohibition."

The Growing Household

Following the judge's advice, Julia did two things. She set about locating Daniel Henry Jones, John's old bodyguard, who had recently been laid off from his offshore job. The offer from Julia could not have come at a better time. Julia had an empty guest cottage near the back of the house. Soon it was readied, and Daniel—D. J.—moved in. His looks were deceiving. A military professional, he was of medium height and build, but he worked out, he studied martial arts, he was familiar with weapons of all sorts, and he could spot a bad guy a mile off. He was 180 pounds of solid muscle. He was a widower, but he had an online girlfriend he had not yet met. She could wait until the situation at Julia's stabilized. D. J. made a suggestion that Julia found to be inspired. Instead of hanging around acting like a bodyguard, he would take on the role of gardener. He enjoyed gardening, loved the outdoors, and would be on constant duty without attracting attention.

"Well, then," Julia replied to the suggestion, "I guess you will get two salaries."

The second thing Julia did was to contact her favorite handyman to get started on a fence. It had to be attractive, but, in Julia's mind, it also had to be sturdy. She wanted steel posts, one-inch-thick boards instead of standard fencing boards, and she wanted it eight feet tall. She would have to find some fast-growing vines to camouflage it and make it look as though it had been there forever. Confederate Jasmine ought to do the trick. She could get the big pots of it and maybe mix in some other vines, and it would be done. There were times when Julia wished she didn't have such a fortune to watch over, but this was not one of them.

Money could make just about anything happen in a hurry when necessity dictated.

In the meantime, Jon Teel showed no inclination to play outside. Julia was grateful for that, because, although she knew children required sunshine, her immediate concern was his physical safety. The DNA results took time, and they did not yet know whether or not the unfortunate murdered woman from Texas was Jon Teel's mother.

A Winding Road

And so it was that Jon Teel arrived at Julia's back door with no fanfare, accompanied by Ronnell Williams, who carried his meager belongings in a brown paper grocery bag. The boy's eyes lit up when he caught sight of Julia, but he looked around at the lavish surroundings of his new home with no sign of emotion. Julia had pulled down the blinds in the sunroom so they would have privacy.

"Are you hungry, Jon Teel?" Julia asked. He shook his head indicating that he was not.

At that moment, the back door burst open, and Florida's two daughters came running in. They stopped instantly when they saw Jon Teel, then walked slowly up to him.

"Hi, Jon Teel. I'm Orlie."

"And I'm Waveland. We are happy to meet you. We want to play with you when you feel like it."

Julia thought she saw a flicker of a smile cross Jon Teel's face, but he made no reply.

"You don't have to say anything, Jon Teel, but we want to show you something we just found. Can we, Mama?"

Florida nodded her acquiescence, and the two girls walked outside, returning moments later with a cardboard box. In it was the tiniest, scrawniest kitten Julia had ever seen. Jon Teel reached into the box, picked up the pitiful creature, and held it to his cheek, "Gato," he said.

Julia was astounded. She had never had an animal in the house, but there was a first time for everything. If a cat was what Jon Teel needed, a cat he would have. Julia and Florida exchanged a look that, for Julia, spoke volumes; the boy had captured Flo's generous heart, the kitten notwithstanding.

"Looks like we will be needing cat food and a litter box. I have never given a cat a bath, but I guess there is a first time for everything," Julia said.

Jon Teel watched and listened but remained quiet, holding onto the newly christened Gato. Florida got down on one knee and spoke quietly to the boy.

"Jon Teel, if you are going to keep that cat, he will have to have a bath. I can see the fleas on his poor little body, and I see some little boo-boos that need attention. Why don't you and the girls come with me to the laundry room and we will get him clean and warm and dry? Julia, don't worry. We can handle this."

To Julia's amazement, Jon Teel got up and followed Florida, one sister on each side of him, staying close but being careful not to touch him.

"Waveland," Florida directed, "go out behind the garden shed and bring me one of those old window screens. I will show you a trick you will never forget about how to bathe a cat."

Soon they were set up around the laundry room sink, Jon Teel still holding on to Gato. Amazingly, the cat seemed to trust the boy, not attempting to escape or to scratch him, even when the water began to flow into the sink. Flo placed an old towel in the bottom of the sink and then leaned the window screen against the side. She took the scruffy kitten and put it on the window screen. Immediately, Gato's claws came out and attached firmly to the squares in the screen. Working quickly, Florida scrubbed the kitten with a soft cloth and mild soap, rinsed him with warm water from the handheld hose, and soon had him wrapped in a warm towel and back in Jon Teel's arms. The kitty began to purr, and a tiny smile crept across the boy's face.

"It can't be this easy," Julia thought as she watched from the doorway.

And it was not—at least not always.

With the business of the cat settled for the moment, Julia took the boy upstairs to show him his room. He wandered through it, looking under the beds and in the closets, but maintaining the robotic composure that, for Julia, had become his signature. Then he pointed to Julia, as though asking if she would share the room and sleep in the other bed.

"Jon, I will show you my room. It is next to this one. If you need me, all you have to do is call and I will come. Or I can give you a little bell to ring. But I will be here all the time."

They walked out into the upstairs hall and into Julia's bedroom. It was furnished with a king-sized bed designed by John. It was an excellent copy of a fine Mallard bed but made to fit a large modern mattress and low enough to be accessible without the small ladder required for many of the antique beds.

Jon Teel looked from the bed to Julia and promptly lay down on the floor under her bed, held the wrapped-up kitten to his chest, and closed his eyes.

Julia was beginning to grasp that she and Jon Teel would be communicating in this peculiar fashion. Julia would speak; Jon Teel would understand perfectly well, but if he answered at all, it would be with a sign or an action. In his new surroundings, he seemed to be afraid of the sound of his own voice. The progress made in his schoolwork did not seem to transfer to his new living arrangement.

"So, Jon, you are telling me that you would rather sleep in here with me?"

He nodded vehemently in the affirmative.

"I believe we can arrange something. But I can't have you sleeping on the floor. We will fix up something better."

Julia decided then and there to throw out the textbooks and the psychology journals and go with her natural instinct. This would not be a straight line from point A to point B. It would be a long and winding road, and the food for this journey would be unremitting, unconditional love.

Slumber Party

Julia knew she had to be particularly careful about sleeping arrangements with Jon Teel. She was documenting everything carefully in a journal on her laptop, giving extra attention to detail in recording Jon's attempt to sleep under her bed. She enlisted D. J.'s help and went up the back stairs to the attic. There, under a dusty sheet, she found what she was seeking: her old walnut youth bed, a bit bigger than a standard baby crib, with sides about a foot tall. The feather mattress had been carefully wrapped in two thicknesses of sheeting. They maneuvered the mattress and then the bed down the winding staircase, turning the bed on end to get it down. It seemed impossible, but it had gotten up there in the first place, so it was bound to come back down.

Florida took over immediately, sending the mattress outdoors with the girls, who were ordered to place it on the picnic table in full sunshine, beat it with a broom, and turn it over every thirty minutes. She cleaned the bed with Murphy's soap and put it in the shade to dry.

When the girls suggested sunshine would dry the bed faster, she replied, "You girls must always remember that hot sun warps wet wood."

Florida was filled with these practical nuggets of valuable information. Julia had long ago realized that Florida had been paying attention to Julia's mother and grandmother all those years while Julia had listened with only half an ear.

Jon Teel had been sitting quietly with Gato on his lap while the bed was being sorted out. Julia had explained what they were doing, and he seemed to understand. If he were going to be one of those victims of child abuse who acted out, it had not manifested itself so far. The kitten was something of a miracle, Julia thought, which reminded her to sit for a moment with a cup of coffee and a wise saying for this momentous day. She sat next to Jon Teel with the big box on her lap and pulled out a long, thin strip that read, "A child is God's proof that the world should continue." With that, she threw caution to the wind and hugged Jon Teel tightly against her side.

"I love you, Jon Teel. I will tell you that every day and I will keep you safe." Although he did not return her hug, he made no attempt to pull away. Julia counted that as progress.

Later that afternoon, D. J., Julia, and Florida got the little bed upstairs and into Julia's bedroom, flush against the side of the big king-sized bed. Orlando and Waveland came dragging the mattress up. They swathed it in fresh linens, placed a pillow at the head, put a soft quilt on top, and even found a little pillow for Gato. Jon Teel looked on but did not touch any of it. The girls kept up constant chatter while all of the action took place. Julia observed that Jon missed nothing of what they said. This was the natural way for him to learn and absorb some of what had been lost in his childhood. The test of all of this elaborate sleeping preparation would come at bedtime.

Julia, together with Orlando, Waveland, Jon Teel, and Gato, spent the rest of the afternoon in Julia's bedroom, bringing in books and toys, playing with the cat, and enjoying the two girls' active imaginations. They loved playacting and soon were wearing Julia's old nightgowns and put a small rhinestone hairclip on the head of poor Gato. He was a good-natured cat, one of those poor strays who knows his good fortune and is happy and grateful to find a home. He allowed them to play with him like a well-treated doll.

At six, the entourage went downstairs, where Florida had sandwiches and fruit for all of them. Jon Teel picked at his food, finally finishing a quarter of a sandwich and a slice of apple. Julia noticed that he seemed to like grapes and bananas and made a note to herself to keep them on hand. Florida announced that tomorrow was Sunday, they would be going to early Mass, and then the three of them would come to stay with Jon Teel while Julia attended the later service. Florida had readily noticed what Julia had: if something were presented to the boy in a quiet, sensible fashion, he readily accepted and went along with it.

Julia then took him upstairs to the bathroom that adjoined his bedroom—she had decided that it would still be his bedroom except for the sleeping arrangement—and drew bathwater for him. When she helped him undress and get into the warm tub, she saw the full extent of the scarring on his frail body. She was overcome with the enormity of the cruelty that had been inflicted upon the boy. She bathed him quickly and got him into his new pajamas. Then she kissed the nub of his missing finger, a gesture that would soon be a habit for Julia. When she checked his teeth after he brushed them, she was happily surprised at their good condition. Someone had at least been trying to care for the child, although not preventing the abuse. Julia wondered if it had been the poor dead woman whose remains were still being examined.

Jon Teel and Gato climbed into the little walnut bed to wait for Julia to get ready for bed in her own bathroom. She decided to skip a shower—she could have one in the morning. She put on pajamas, brushed her teeth, and climbed into her own bed, sliding over next to Jon Teel's bed.

"Jon," she asked, "do you say your prayers?"

She was surprised when he nodded yes.

"Let's pray together, then. I am thanking God for bringing you to me."

They made the sign of the cross and Julia said the Our Father. Then she said her favorite prayer, the one to St. Michael the Archangel. If ever she needed a saint and an angel to defend her in battle, it was now. She had a bad feeling that there was much more to come before the child's life was settled and secure. For now, he needed to begin to feel at home. The first thing Monday morning, she would set about organizing her troops, circling the wagons, and manning the ramparts—whatever she could do to protect her little fortress.

She snuggled down into her big bed, suddenly realizing how tired she was. She rolled onto her side to look through the railing at Jon Teel. Solemn black eyes stared back at her, disconcerting her for a moment. She reached between the railing bars and patted his hand. He clutched her hand with a ferocity that said, "Do not let me go!" She held on to the tiny hand until he closed his eyes. Gato slept above his head, purring as loudly as an old refrigerator.

Julia looked up at the crucifix above her bedroom door.

"Jesus," she said, "no one told me it could be like this. From the bottom of my heart, thank you!" Silent tears of gratitude slid down her cheeks, and she continued to hold the tiny, warm brown hand until she fell asleep.

Meanwhile, to the West

A nondescript, mud-spattered gray Nissan Altima pulled into the huge parking lot of the Buc-ee's convenience store on I-10 north of Baytown. The car drove slowly around the concrete expanse, aiming for a spot away from the front entrance and just out of range of the video surveillance cameras monitoring the place day and night.

The occupants sat in silence for a while, engine idling and AC blowing cold air into the confined space. Finally the driver, a huge black man, spoke.

"Boss, how long you think it's gonna take them to get here?"

The passenger, a thin, lighter skinned man with a moustache, replied.

"Shouldn't be much longer. They checked in from Beaumont a good while ago. I told them no speeding, no nothing to attract the police. That car stands out enough as it is. But I wanted it seen in Louisiana with those two guys driving it. I wanted it noticed."

He spoke in an oddly inflected English, more proper than his companion, with a hint of foreign influence. His language was laced with far less profanity than his friend's.

"Boss, I don't know your plan, but I know you got one, and I know it'll work out. It always does."

At that moment, a low-slung, metallic red muscle car rumbled into the parking spot next to the Nissan. Two men got out and entered the back seat of the Nissan.

"Hope you got the right news for me, boys," the mustachioed man said.

"See for yourself, Boss," the shorter of the newcomers said, handing over a high-end Canon camera with a long-range lens.

On the viewing screen on the back of the camera was a clear image of a woman exiting the rear entrance of Dapplefield Manor, holding the hand of a young boy.

"No doubt about it, Boss. It's Jon Teel. We hung around that town for several days, going in and out. We stayed at a place on the highway in Lafayette so we wouldn't get in no trouble in Bakerville, but the damn cops stopped us twice. Wasn't doing nuthin'. We had our licenses, our insurance, everything. The only problem might be the car is in your name, but they didn't seem to make us on that. Just the usual locals hasslin' someone from out of town. Boss, I felt nekkid without a gun, but you were right about that and you been right about keeping that car clean. Those dumb shits searched every inch of the car and brought in the drug dog, but they couldn't find nuthin'. But that lady, she keeps the boy inside most of the time. This is the first time we seen him. Her house is big, and plenty people in and out. It's gonna be tough to grab him."

"Won't be any need for grabbing him. He is my boy, and I'm going to go and take what is mine. If they had anything on us, they would have been knocking on our door a long time ago. But Anthony, just tell me one more time *exactly* what his no-good momma said before you finished with her? I gotta figure out what she was talking about."

"Well, Boss," he smirked, "while she could still talk, she said, 'You can beat me and you can kill me, but I will never tell you where I took my son. And he has an insurance. I wrote it for him. They will find it if you try to hurt him.' I think she was trying to say 'an insurance policy,'" Anthony said, "and after that, I finished with her and she wasn't doin' no talking."

"Okay. Those sumbitches would have been here by now if they had anything. The coroner doesn't have a clue who that body is. I think it's time we make a little trip to Bakerville. I can be as nice and proper as those rich people, but I know how to take care of business before they know what hit 'em," Moustache said.

"We all goin', Boss?" This was from the fourth man, a tall, muscular guy with poorly done tattoos covering his forearms, the work of a Huntsville cellmate.

"No, I don't want to attract any more attention than necessary. I am going to get my own child. If anybody asks, his mother abused him and then took off with him, and I have no idea where she went. I am a grieving father looking for his only child."

With that, the other three erupted in raucous laughter. While the others laughed in genuine amusement, Moustache's smile never reached his eyes. He held up a hand for silence.

"Not a laughing matter, boys. Beast and I will take care of this. It's going to take me a few days to organize the details. No room for error. It has to go right the first time. You two will stay at the shed and hold down the fort. If anybody asks, I'm away on business. It will be time soon. Everything will go on as usual, deliveries and collections on schedule. Okay, let's roll. I've got a trip and a reunion party to plan."

Peaceful Interlude

At Mass the next day, Julia prayed for clarity and strength. She needed the clarity to see what needed to be done and the strength to carry it through. Jon Teel, she decided, needed physical and emotional protection first and an education second. Julia had decided with the approval of Porteous Green and Hannah Clarkson that, given the unusual nature of Jon Teel's case and given his lack of success at Carter Elementary, she would homeschool him. The principal at Carter was particularly grateful. She was not equipped to deal with the boy, and she did not need his abusive parent to appear at her door.

Julia had decided that she would be informal in the beginning, allowing the child to learn through the kind of play he had never been allowed to enjoy. Florida's girls would help, and they took to the task with gusto. On Sunday afternoons, they played board games, memory card games, sorting games, and counting games. They taught him shapes and colors. The boy had a sharp mind; Julia had witnessed it many times. He could tally up the total number of buttons of different colors sorted into a muffin tin before his two young teachers arrived at the answer. They praised him beyond all reason, and he soaked it in like a neglected petunia that suddenly gets a good watering. He beamed. This told Julia that someone had taught him something besides how to pray and how to brush his teeth. He still spoke very little, but Julia was sure that would come. She had the feeling that he had been taught from a very young age to be still and silent or suffer terrible consequences.

*   *   *   *   *

On a Monday morning, Julia had an appointment with Porteous Green and Sheriff Blanchard at the insistence of the sheriff. She asked if D. J. and Jamal could be included. Florida would watch Jon Teel. They met in the judge's chambers, with Porteous insisting that each of them enter separately, several minutes apart, through the back door. There were trustees working on the grounds—inmates on work release—and Porteous obviously trusted no one. Julia and Jamal were both regular visitors to the judge, so they would raise few eyebrows, and no one knew D. J., but it paid to be overly cautious. In the criminal world, there was no telling who knew whom or who observed and reported.

The sheriff began.

"First, I am deputizing all of you. You, too, Miss Julia. Second, I am solemnly swearing you to secrecy. What I am going to tell you here cannot leave this room. We have the DNA match on the woman found murdered and left in the water in Texas. There is no doubt that she is the mother of our boy. She got caught up as a mule at the age of fourteen hauling drugs up through Matamoras to Corpus Christi and on to Houston. Her daddy sold her to the local cartel to save the rest of his family. She was a pretty thing, smart, and she caught the eye of the Jefe in the Houston area. That's as much as I know on that front—no name, no description yet on the man—but I can tell you this: the sheriff over there is a sharp guy who knows he has a mole going straight to these lowlifes. When the coroner finished with the body, the sheriff had him publish his findings as probable homicide of an unknown subject, possibly a Mexican national. Then, he and the coroner got a big old dog carcass, zipped it up in a body bag, had a makeshift but much publicized funeral for the poor unknown drowned girl, and sent the old hound dog off for cremation. The real remains are in Baton Rouge with our extremely savvy criminal anthropologist."

"Has she released any findings?" Julia could not refrain from asking.

"Only one thing of very particular interest to us. The dead woman had a missing little finger that may actually have been bitten off. She is still working on it, and she has only bone to work with, but she is pretty sure. She is hoping for a tooth mark but that will be tough."

This was greeted by stunned silence until the sheriff added, "She also thinks a human mouth did the biting."

Julia felt that she might be sick but managed to control her roiling stomach.

"Sheriff," she said, "I can hardly bring myself to ask, but has she compared it with the X-rays of Jon Teel's hand?"

The judge answered the question.

"That brings us to the next point. This has to be by the book and beyond. These slimy creatures tend to have the best legal counsel unlimited funds can provide. We need to access Jon Teel's X-rays, and even though we may not need it, I want a warrant to do it. Julia, you are his legal guardian. If you and I both sign for his X-rays and we ask for the whole batch of them using the excuse that you are consulting with another doctor, I think we can get by with it without raising an eyebrow. I will talk to the doc myself, but I will also make sure he has the legal papers just in case. I will have the doctor seal the X-rays in an unlabeled envelope, and I will pick them up when I go in for my blood pressure check tomorrow. Then I will drop them off in Baton Rouge on my way to a meeting the next day."

Jamal spoke up. "You fellows are scaring the wits out of me for Miss Julia. She has put herself into what appears to me to be a very dangerous situation to protect this child. We have to keep her and the boy safe, whatever it takes."

"And we will, J-Max," the sheriff said. "We will know if any of the dirt bags cross the Sabine River. They have to realize the child is alive and can identify them. If they have half a brain, they will leave well enough alone. But these guys do not like to leave loose ends. We will be ready, though, starting with an assessment later today of Miss Julia's home. We have to have a plan in place, just like a tornado drill. Jon Teel must learn to use the safe room without hesitation. And Miss Julia, you need to learn to use a serious handgun."

The planning session continued. A person trusted by the sheriff installed security cameras and a special signal with activation buttons hidden unobtrusively throughout the house. It also activated a flashing red beacon atop the widow's walk on the roof of Dapplefield Manor. The signal light was easily visible from the courthouse, which housed the sheriff's office.

As was the case with most old homes of its era, Dapplefield Manor had two stairways. In the front entry hall, there was a grand staircase leading to the second floor, featuring huge carved balusters, delicate spindles, massive newel posts, and carpet held in place with brass rods at the back of each tread. At the rear of the house, hidden behind a plain door at the end of hall, was the back stairway. Rising steeply in a near-circular fashion, these were the working stairs of the home. Laundry, chamber pots, and morning coffee, all the mundane household conveniences, traversed this stairway in the old days when there were many servants and no indoor plumbing.

During the days of Prohibition, Julia's grandfather, the first Judge Chandler, had tried several bootleggers in his courtroom. He was threatened, with shots fired into the walls of Dapplefield Manor late one night. He decided to make use of the wasted space beneath the back stairway to construct a hidden safe room. He put in two points of entry. The first was a small door cleverly hidden in the wainscoting around the bottom of the stairway near the pantry at the back of the downstairs hall. The second point of entry was a wooden, carpet-covered stair tread just below the second landing of the staircase. It opened by simply lifting the step upward. There was a ladder attached to the inside wall of the small space to facilitate quick entry. The stair tread could be propped up and held open by means of a sturdy board that fit into a groove on the inside edge of the tread. Both doors could be locked securely from the inside, and both were practically invisible from the outside. Julia hoped they would never actually need the tiny room.

Jon Teel not only learned to use the safe room hidden beneath the back stairway, he absolutely loved it. He never entered it without Gato. It was stocked with bottled water, packaged food, cat food, a litter box, and a sleeping bag. There was a vent connected to the heating and air conditioning system coming from under the floor, and there was a small portable toilet. Jon Teel willingly practiced until he could enter from the first-floor door or from the door that doubled as a stair step. He never questioned Julia about the need for the safe room; Julia felt that stealth and secrecy had always been a part of his survival.

*   *   *   *   *

Meanwhile, Jon Teel's lessons were progressing. Julia tried her best to maintain a semblance of normalcy and routine. The boy was reading on a first-grade level, but his math skills were off the charts. Julia prepared simple science experiments. Jon Teel looked forward to science days. He was still reticent about speaking and did not warm up to strangers, but because his life was so sheltered, few strangers came into their orbit.

Their days fell into an easy routine that both Julia and the boy enjoyed. To placate her card-playing buddies and to give Jon a break from her, Julia spent one afternoon a week playing gin. She varied the day, following the sheriff's advice, so that if anyone were watching, they could not predict her comings and goings.

One week, with the permission of the sheriff, she invited the card players to her home. She enlisted Orlie and Waveland to babysit upstairs, but she instructed them to bring Jon Teel down to meet the ladies when they arrived.

Julia could have hugged them all. They arrived en masse with Myrtle leading the way, laden with gifts for Jon Teel. Julia instantly regretted cutting them out of her life to the extent that she had, particularly since she could not reveal the reason nor the danger she might be in.

"You are my truest, dearest friends," she began, calling upstairs for the girls to bring Jon Teel down.

The child said nothing but managed a smile as the ladies cooed over him. Julia did not miss the exchanged looks and raised eyebrows among them, but waited until the children were upstairs and they were at the card tables to broach the delicate subject.

"Look, my old friends, let's not pussyfoot around this elephant in the room. Yes, I have become a foster parent—officially—to Jon Teel. Porteous Green asked me to tutor him, and yes I became attached. Maybe I have unfulfilled mothering desires. Maybe I feel I have a lot to offer such a child. I know it is really, really asking a lot, but I must swear you to secrecy regarding the child."

"But Julia," Margot said, "you know that's wishful thinking. People know you have the child, and people do talk whether you want them to or not. We didn't think this was a good idea on any number of levels—we made no bones about it. But you are our friend, and we love you, and this is something you obviously want to do."

"What Margot is trying to say in her long-winded fashion is that we've got your back," Louella barked.

The cards were forgotten and the old friends regaled one another with old stories and laughter such as they had not enjoyed since the arrival of Jon Teel. Once they all departed in Louella's long black Cadillac, Julia leaned against the front door to gather her composure. She walked into the office where she found Florida poring over a ledger and paying bills. She bent down and grabbed her friend and confidante.

"Flo," she whispered, "I finally think we are going to get through this nightmare and come out on the other side."

Biding Time

Through these long weeks, Jamal—J-Max—was a regular visitor, earning the trust of Jon Teel in record time. They roughhoused outside in the enclosed fence, which Julia thought was a fine activity for the boy. He needed fresh air, sunshine, and exercise. J-Max and D. J. were good for him, as were Orlie and Waveland. Julia wished he could be in a regular school classroom, but she had faith that day would come.

*   *   *   *   *

Julia knew in her heart that she was continuing to make great progress with the boy. He was comfortable with her now; he seemed at home. The decision to homeschool him was the correct one, in fact the only way. Julia was certain of this. He continued to blossom under her one-on-one tutelage, revealing the powerful intellect behind the sad brown eyes and the shy demeanor.

"I must do something to get him out of this house," she thought, "the occasional playtime in the fenced yard is not enough. He needs to feel like a normal kid and walk down the street once in a while." She continued to mull this over, but took no action.

Then one day, from his upstairs bedroom window, Jon Teel spied a strange automobile drive slowly past the house and circle back to pass by again. It was a car that was easy to remember: florescent red metallic paint with flames behind the wheel covers, low-slung body, and menacing hubcaps with dagger-like projections. Its darkened windows prevented any identification of the occupants, and Julia was unable to read the license plate from her vantage point. Jon Teel had crawled beneath Julia's bed and had to be coaxed out after seeing the vehicle, but he would not answer any question about the car. "Beast," his standard response to everything bad, was all that he would say. Florida, at the curb taking out trash, had seen the vehicle and noted that it was a Texas plate and got the last three digits. Julia called the sheriff to report the occurrence, then tried to put it out of her mind. A few weeks passed, and the car did not reappear. Julia decided to follow her heart instead of her head and take the boy out for a short walk.

"Jon," she said, "I thought we would get outside. You have asked me about the church that you see from your bedroom window. Would you like to see it while no one is there? I think you would enjoy it."

Julia had been longing to take the child to Mass with her, to walk right down to a front pew and show him off as all her friends showed off their children and grandchildren when they visited. She thanked God for the gift of this child in her life, but she was afraid the big congregation would be too much for him. They would make an odd pair on Sunday: the lonely, wealthy lady of the manor and the oddly beautiful biracial mystery child. Julia was well past caring what people thought. The boy had laid claim to her heart. She had discussed formal adoption with Porteous Green. She thought of Jon Teel as her own. Though some months remained before the judge could permanently sever the legal rights of the unknown father, they had discussed the serious possibility of the adoption of the child Jon Teel by the widow Julia Chandler Hancock.

* * * * *

Most of the main events in the tapestry of Julia's life had been woven in the venerable old Catholic church on Main Street. She had been baptized there and received the sacraments of penance and the Eucharist, and there she had buried both of her parents. John had asked for her hand in marriage sitting in a front pew after Mass one Sunday, and they had married a few weeks later in the church. And there she had laid her beloved John to rest.

Jon Teel nodded his agreement to go to the church. As Julia helped him with his jacket, she wondered again at the strange, rough scars encircling his wrists. She brought his left hand to her lips and once again kissed the tiny stub of the missing finger. Then they stepped out onto the sidewalk. Heavy clouds like bags full of bayou water hung heavy in the sky, but the weatherman had said there would be no rain. A front would push through shortly, bringing relief from the leaden air. A lazy gust of wind rustled the moss-draped oaks on Julia's front lawn.

They walked quickly to the church and entered through the main door. Another gust of wind blew through the door as they entered. The church was dark, but their eyes soon adjusted. Suddenly, the clouds on the southwest side of the church parted. A shaft of brilliant sunlight pierced the magnificent demi-lune stained glass Crucifixion window high over the altar, momentarily mesmerizing Julia once again with its beauty. All the colors of the finest Renaissance art glowed with a heavenly light.

She looked down to see if Jon had noticed. His small face was transformed, his eyes alight. He walked slowly up the aisle, eyes fixed on the figure of the crucified Christ. When he reached the end of the main aisle, he fell to his knees and stretched his arms straight out, a perfect imitation of the figure on the cross.

Realization dawned in Julia's horrified mind. She reached for one of his arms, pushed the jacket sleeve up, and pointed to the scar encircling his wrist, then to the figure in the stained glass window.

"Jon, is this—"

The boy nodded, tears starting down his cheeks, the first tears he had shed since he had come to live with Julia.

She drew him to her side and went to the front pew, where they sat together. Julia's first reaction was an anger so ferocious that she could have, at that moment, killed in cold blood the person responsible for Jon Teel's suffering. Then she looked up at the Crucifixion window and tried to remember what it was all about, redemption and forgiveness.

"Jon Teel," she said, throwing caution to the wind, "let's pray for your mama, and then let's pray for the people that hurt you. Maybe God can help them to be better and not be so mean."

Jon Teel fixed his unblinking black eyes on Julia's face and nodded. Then he knelt down and made the sign of the cross, adding the extra little touch to the forehead and the lips that she had seen the faithful do in Spanish churches. Julia followed suit, saying the Our Father aloud for the two of them. Then they again made the sign of the cross, got up, and left the church. Jon Teel turned to gaze back at the stained glass window several times as they made their way back up the long aisle.

Hell Breaks Loose

Florida was waiting at the door for Julia when they returned.

"Julia, the sheriff has called three times, and J-Max is on the way over. Something is going to happen, and it sounds like it will be soon. D. J. went to New Iberia for the rest of the plants and the mulch, but the sheriff got hold of him, and he is headed back. What do you want me to do?"

"Flo, I want you to do exactly as we have planned. I want you to go to St. John and pick up your girls and take them home and lock your doors. You are not their target, and there is nothing you can do here. Your duty is to protect your girls. Now, I feel certain that we are being watched. Just get your purse and get into your car as though everything is totally normal. Drive on over to St. John. Go on. There is no time to spare."

Then she instructed Jon Teel to take Gato and get into the safe room. The boy obeyed immediately but turned back and pointed to Julia as though asking her to join him in the place of refuge.

"No, Jon, I will be fine. J-Max, the sheriff, and D. J. will be here to help me."

With Florida out of harm's way, Julia called the sheriff.

"Julia, I have a feeling it is all going down today," the sheriff began without fanfare. "Are you ready for this? I haven't told you, but that devil red car has been in and out of town for several days. Problem is, it's just some low-level thugs scoping things out. This morning, our law enforcement buddies in Texas got word to us that the big baddie, one Jonathan Reynoldo Steelman, a.k.a. The Steel Man, is headed our way in that very same vehicle, which is registered to him. And guess who's the driver? A big muscle man known as Beast. Steelman got a Texas driver's license with a Social Security number from a deceased person, so we have no idea who he really is. Near as we can figure, Beast is a career criminal whose real name is Samuel Burleson. He will be up for three strikes if we can convict him. But Julia, short of having Jon Teel testify, I don't know how we will do it. Where there's a will, there's a way, though, and if ever there were two worthless pieces of scum that need to be taken down, these two are it."

Julia let that sink in for a minute. She decided she was ready. This limbo had to end, and she could do whatever it took. The names Beast and Jonathan Steelman could not be coincidence. Jon Teel blamed his missing finger on Beast, and Jonathan Steelman could certainly abbreviate to Jon Teel.

"Jon Teel is in the safe room. I don't see how they can know of its existence. J-Max should be here any minute and D. J. too. Have your guys gotten in place across the street?" Julia was thinking as fast as she could, trying not to let fear take hold.

"Yes, we are set. We even have a crack marksman up in the church steeple. I am going to station one deputy out of sight behind your garden shed with a video camera feed of your back door area. You will never be alone even though it may seem that way. Our best case scenario is that you and D. J. sit outside at the table under the oak tree like you're having a morning cup of coffee and planning his work in the gardens for the day. Our ace in the hole will be J-Max. He will be out of sight just inside your back door. I have made him break his rule. He is armed with a sawed-off shotgun and a handgun for good measure. We think the Texas pair is going to show up. Steelman has been making noises around an undercover narc about going to Louisiana to get his boy back. Problem we have is, we have no proof whatsoever that he is the one who hurt Jon Teel. Short of having the boy face him and testify, we are going to have to do three things. First, we need a DNA sample so we will know without a doubt that he is the father of your boy. Second, we need a confession or some other proof that he is the abuser. And third, we need to get both of these lowlifes into custody with a minimum of bloodshed. Are you sure you are in? Because we could simply arrest them on trumped-up charges, but I am afraid they will be out in hours and this will not reach any kind of conclusion."

"Sheriff, I would trust Jamal with my life. Let's play it out like we rehearsed and see where it goes," Julia said.

* * * * *

On the west side of town, the red vehicle stopped at a gas station in the curve approaching the cemetery.

"All right, Beast. Showtime. Live up to your name if you have to. You know what to do. Walk through the cemetery like you are visiting your long-lost dead family. If anybody is there, it will be jailhouse trustees mowing grass, and they know to look the other way. Just make your way to the bayou, and you are going to find a nice little boat with a quiet trolling motor. It's a short trip up the bayou to that rich woman's castle. Tie up out of sight and make your way up the yard. There is bound to be somebody up there watching, but they will be watching the house, not the bayou. Just take care of them however you have to. You know what to do. I'll try to get the woman away, but if I don't, you take care of her, too, and get in that house and get my boy."

Julia and D. J. situated themselves outside the back door at a wrought iron table set up on the grass, each with a cup of coffee and a section of the morning paper, as though it were the most natural activity in the world—which it was. D. J. had a notepad on which he was listing gardening chores that needed tending. They were not there long when the shiny red muscle car sidled up into the driveway. A thin man of medium height got out of the car, apparently alone, holding a plastic bottle of water in one hand and a heavy gold link key chain in the other. Julia's mind instantly registered several things: the man resembled Jon Teel, he was a mixture of African American and some other ethnicity, and he was the embodiment of Satan himself. He stood about ten feet from Julia and D. J.

D. J. stood up.

"Good morning," he said politely, the picture of genial good nature. "I am Mrs. Hancock's gardener. What can we do for you this beautiful day?"

If the visitor was taken aback by the friendly, open greeting, he did not let on.

He took a big swig from his water bottle, making a point of being in no hurry to accommodate them, then tossed the bottle on the side of the driveway, disdainful of Julia's property.

"I have recently learned that the woman who lives in this house has something of mine, and I have come to get it back. She has my son. I have come to take him back to Texas, where he belongs."

"Whoa, whoa," D. J. replied. "Mrs. Julia has been serving as a foster mother to a child at the request of the court, nothing more. We can call the judge and get this all sorted out. The child isn't here now anyhow. He is off with the social worker for a psych evaluation." He paused for the effect of the psych evaluation to sink in. "I recommend that the three of us get in that fine automobile of yours and head over to the courthouse and talk to the judge. If you have the proper credentials, you can probably get your boy today. By the way, I didn't catch your name."

"I am Jonathan Steelman," moustache replied.

"And I am Julia Hancock," Julia said.

Steelman began to toss the gold key chain up into the air, catching it behind his back. It was a trick that must have taken hours to perfect.

"Won't be any need for involving the law. My boy is here, he is my blood, and he will leave this place with me now, by whatever means necessary."

Suddenly, J-Max revealed himself, his massive presence appearing in the doorway, very near to Steelman. J-Max was resplendent in his uniform. Steelman, apparently unfazed, continued to toss the key chain in the air, catching it each time. With lightning speed, J-Max unclipped the nightstick from his belt and pressed the button, extending the metal baton out to catch the key ring in midair. He lowered the heavy key chain down the stick and into his huge palm. For a moment, Steelman was thunderstruck, still looking around for the keys. J-Max examined the key chain with interest. Among the attachments on it were a gold skull and crossbones and two curved, stick-like objects that looked like the dried brown claws of a good-sized bird.

"Now," J-Max said, showing his open, friendly television personality smile, "why don't the three of us get into this fine automobile I've been itching to drive and mosey on over to the courthouse. The judge can check out your paperwork, get the boy brought over to you, and you can be on your way."

Steelman was not about to get caught in a trap.

"No need to involve Mrs. Hancock," he said. "Let's just leave her here in case that social worker brings my boy back, and you and I can go talk to the judge." With that, he headed for the passenger side of the car.

J-Max gave Julia a look, but she nodded and said, "I certainly do think D. J. and I should wait here for Jon Teel. Go ahead, Jamal, and take Mr. Steelman down to the courthouse."

J-Max and Steelman drove away. Julia had the eerie feeling that she was a tiny bird with the paw of a big cat on its neck. Something was off. She hoped the deputies were alert.

*   *   *   *   *

Through the cattails on the bayou side, a boat silently glided up to the shore. Not chancing an easy exit onto the dock, Beast stepped into the shallow water, cursing under his breath that he hadn't thought to change his good shoes, and made his way to shore. For a man of gigantic proportions, he could move swiftly and silently. He could see the deputy stationed by the garden shed, engrossed in watching the video feed on his smartphone. In seconds, Beast grabbed him from behind and knocked him out with a ham-fisted blow to the head.

Julia and D. J., meanwhile, had gone back into the house, afraid to check on Jon Teel in the safe room for fear that Steelman would return but also afraid to leave him alone.

"Miss Julia," D. J. said, "I'm going to go out the front door and walk the perimeter. With your oak trees in the way, there is not a clear view from the church, and I'm worried about someone getting around the wood fence unseen."

"Oh, yes, good idea," Julia said automatically. "I'll stay inside."

D. J. slipped silently out the front door as Julia paced nervously, glad that she had sent Florida and her girls out of harm's way. She knew the sheriff must be nearby, but she wished she knew where.

A sharp knock at the back door caused her to jump.

"Miss Julia, it's the deputy. Can you come check something out here?"

Julia ran to the back door and opened it. Beast, waiting around the side of the doorjamb, grabbed her around the waist and slammed her head against the brick wall. She slumped to the brick pavers, unconscious.

Beast ran through the back door and up the center hall, calling, "Jon Teel, Jon Teel, you better come out. You know I will find you. I always do. The longer it takes, the madder I'm gonna be."

He made it to the front of the hall and bounded up the main staircase.

"Jon Teel, this ain't gonna be pretty, boy. I been missing you. You better show yourself. I know you're here."

He checked out each bedroom, then saw a closed door at the end of the upstairs hall. Opening it, he discovered the back stairway winding down to the first floor. He started down, sure now that he was homing in on his helpless quarry.

"Jon Teel! Jon Teel! I'm getting close. I can smell you, boy!"

Jon Teel, listening in his hideaway beneath the steps, heard each footfall. Just then, Gato let out a loud, pitiful meow. Beast paused, listening intently, then continued down. At exactly the right moment, when Beast reached the stair tread above the trapdoor, Jon Teel opened the hidden door from below, pushing it up with the board used to prop the hidden door open. He managed to fit the board into the groove to hold it securely. Taken by surprise, Beast tripped over the obstacle, falling with the full force of his great bulk down the curving steps, around the landing, and out the door at the bottom, where D. J. and the sheriff were waiting for him.

They handcuffed the huge man and added leg shackles for good measure. Then the deputy gave the signal. Vehicles and sirens approached from every direction. Not wanting Jon Teel to catch sight of Beast, D. J. went up the stairway and helped him climb up the ladder, Gato clutched under his arm. He was trembling, but he was smiling.

"I did good, huh, Mr. D. J.?" If D. J. was surprised to hear the boy speak, he did not let on.

"Yes, Jon Teel. You did good."

Tears were flowing from the big man's eyes as he hugged the boy and cat together.

Julia, meanwhile, was being treated in the driveway for a probable concussion and broken ribs. After Beast was taken away, Jon Teel made his way to Julia's side. Together, they rode by ambulance to the hospital. Gato waited in Jon Teel's room.

*　*　*　*

At the courthouse, Porteous Green was playing the genial, cooperative judge anxious to get the poor child back with his father until word came in the form of a message whispered through the door of the judge's chambers. Mission accomplished. The judge's demeanor changed in the time it took him to turn around.

"Well, now, Mr. Steelman, or whatever the hell your name is, apparently your run of good luck has come to an end."

Two armed deputies appeared in the doorway.

"We have your DNA from your water bottle. It will take some time, but we believe it will show that you are the father of the boy Jon Teel. We also have your keychain, which has attached two dried human fingers. The DNA should not be hard to match there either. We believe one to be the missing finger of our young friend Jon Teel and the other to be that of his mother, the unfortunate murdered girl, Maria Maristella Lopez, of Saltillo, Mexico. It may take a while, but it will be easy to prove all of this and the abuse inflicted on the child."

"You can prove nothing," Steelman said. "His mother is the one who abused him. I threatened to turn her in, and she ran away with the child. I am a poor innocent father deprived of his own offspring."

The judge made no reply to Steelman but ordered the deputies to take him away. They could hold him for seventy-two hours on the strength of what his man Beast had done to Julia, which constituted attempted murder. The sheriff came in, and the two conferred.

"You know," Sheriff Blanchard said, "he has a point. We have got to have more or he is going to walk. Let's go over to the hospital and talk to Julia and the boy. One avenue to explore might be the bite marks. If the man Beast actually did bite off the fingers of Jon Teel and his mother, our gal in Baton Rouge ought to be able to prove it."

Jon Teel was sitting on the bed with Julia in the emergency room. Now that he was certain that Beast and Steelman were in custody, the floodgates opened up, and Jon Teel began to speak.

"Mami told me not to talk. Not to talk to anyone, or I could die. So I did not talk. Her friend told her about Auntie. She told me Auntie would be my mama, but Auntie died. Now Julia is hurt. But Mami, is she okay or is she dead? She told me she might not see me again. If anything happened to Mami, you have got to find my books."

They all looked at one another, at a loss.

"My books. The ones that were in my bag, on the bus."

Sirens blaring, the sheriff made it to his office in record time. He picked up the evidence bag, taking a deputy along to preserve the chain of evidence. When they returned to the emergency room, Julia looked much better, although her head was bandaged and her ribs were taped. The bad guys were caught; all was right with the world. A headache and some broken ribs were a small price to pay.

"Okay, Jon Teel. Let's see what these books have to give us," the sheriff said.

He put the two books into the boy's small hands. One was a *Little Golden Book* called *Birds of All Kinds*. No wonder the child had shocked Julia one afternoon at the bayou side, correctly naming a great blue heron. The second book was titled, *My First Counting Book*. On the cover were three kittens, one of them a dead ringer for Gato. Without hesitating, Jon Teel opened the cover of the tattered book. The discarded library book still had a card pocket glued inside, from the days before computer cataloguing. Jon Teel reached a tiny forefinger into the pocket and drew out a paper, folded many times. It was covered with hand-printed words.

It began, "In case of my death—"

As the sheriff quickly scanned the miniscule printing, he looked up, smiled, and said,

"The mother lode."

The paper described a well-hidden headquarters in a boathouse in sight of the San Jacinto monument outside of Houston and very near to I-10. With the landmarks she provided, it should be easy for Texas law enforcement officers to locate. More importantly, her account named names—both those working under Steelman and those who had been murdered along the way. Jon Teel's mother had been locked up and abused, but she had been listening, remembering, and recording. She described in detail what Steelman promised to do to her if she took his son and ran away, and the exact injuries she described were revealed in her skeletal remains. The English was not grammatically correct, but Jon Teel's mother had been intelligent and resourceful and had managed to save her son when she could not save herself.

Julia could hear no more. She drifted off into a blessed, drug-induced sleep. Jon Teel stroked her hand and whispered, "Te amo, Julia. Mami nueva."

Acknowledgments

My heartfelt thanks to all who read this manuscript as it evolved, offering suggestions and encouragement. Special thanks to Kim Graham, Suzanne Wiltz, and Diane Dempsey Legnon, whose written notes and critiques were invaluable.

Front Cover Art Lana Laws Downing

Back Cover Photograph Robbie Keller Le Blanc

Black and White Drawings Laura Zuniga

Ferguson, Walter. Birds of All Kinds. New York: Golden Press, 1959.

Moore, Lilian. My First Counting Book. New York: Golden Book, 1956.

About the Author

Lana Laws Downing writes fiction and nonfiction from her home in South Louisiana.

CPSIA information can be obtained
at www.ICGtesting.com
Printed in the USA
BVHW06s1550310518
517875BV00004B/30/P